Early Indian Village Churches

Early Indian Village Churches

WOODEN FRONTIER ARCHITECTURE IN BRITISH COLUMBIA

John Veillette and Gary White

COMMENTARIES BY

Harold Kalman, Robin Fisher, Warren Sommer

University of British Columbia Press

VANCOUVER

Early Indian Village Churches
© 1977 The University of British Columbia
all rights reserved

Canadian Cataloguing in Publication Data

Veillette, John, 1948-
    Early Indian village churches

    Bibliography: p.
    ISBN 0-7748-0074-7 bd.
    ISBN 0-7748-0075-5 pa.

    1. Rural churches — British Columbia.
2. Church architecture — British Columbia.
3. Indians of North America — British
Columbia — Missions. I. White, Gary, 1940-
II. Title.

NA5246.B7V44   726'.5'09711   C77-002182-4

International Standard Book Number 0-7748-0074-7 (hard cover)
                                                0-7748-0075-5 (paper cover)
Printed in Canada

To the faithful departed

This book has been published with the help of a gift to scholarly publishing made in honour of Dr. Harold S. Foley for his distinguished services to The University of British Columbia, and grants from:
Dr. Walter H. Gage
The Canada Council
The McLean Foundation

Contents

Photo Credits

If credit is not listed, photos are those of the authors. Numbers given are those of the pages on which photos appear.

t — top, b — bottom, l — left, r — right

Photos on 1, 2, 7b, 9, 31, 33, 41t, 49, 62t, 65b, 79t, 87l, 88, 108t, 134br, 156b, and 165t appear courtesy of the British Columbia Provincial Museum.

Photos on 5, 6, 7t, 13, 36b, 47, 52t, 52b, 55t, 55b, 57t, 57b, 58, 60b, 61t, 63t, 63b, 64, 90b, 98b, 107b, 120t, and 173b are reproduced courtesy of the Provincial Archives of British Columbia.

Photos on 8, 10, 56t, 56b, 59, 61b, 66b, and 70bl are courtesy of the Diocese of Caledonia.

Photo on 27 is courtesy of the Glenbow-Alberta Institute, Calgary.

Photo on 32t is courtesy of the United Church of Canada, B.C. Conference Archives and the Centennial Museum, Vancouver.

Photos on 34t, 34b, 35t, 35b, 36t, 40, and 41b are reproduced courtesy of the Vancouver Public Library.

Photo on 38t appears courtesy of the City Archives, City Hall, Vancouver (In. N. 50, P. 100).

Photos on 43t and 43b are courtesy of Mr. Norman M. Carter.

Photos on 48t and 48b appear courtesy of Mr. Peter MacNair.

Photos on 50 and 51 are reproduced courtesy of Mt. Angel Abbey, St. Benedict, Oregon.

Photo on 60t appears courtesy of the American Museum of National History.

Photo on 62b is courtesy of the *Vancouver Sun*.

Photo on 66t is reproduced courtesy of Father John Blyth.

Photo on 68 appears courtesy of the estate of the late Miss Katie O'Neill.

Photo on 70t is courtesy of Mr. James Fowler.

Photo on 76 appears courtesy of Public Archives of Canada (PA45148).

Photo on 78t is courtesy of *War Cry* (21 November 1959).

Photo on 78b is courtesy of Mr. Peter H. E. Botham.

Photos on 86t, 86b, and 89 are courtesy of Mr. Warren Sommer.

Photos on 127t and 127b appear courtesy of Mr. Don W. Yeaman.

Photo on 130t is reproduced courtesy of Mr. and Mrs. Tommy Adolph.

Photo on 156t is courtesy of the South Cariboo Historical Museum Society.

Photo on 173t is from A. G. Morice, *Fifty Years in Western Canada* (Toronto, 1930).

Foreword

The motorist who travels the byways of British Columbia often catches a glimpse of a dignified old frame church standing along the side of the road. The building may show obvious signs of disuse: belfry askew, eaves sagging, windows broken, a few clapboards missing, a pile of debris nearby. The structure is probably an Indian mission church from an earlier age: a pathetic and perhaps unwilling survivor of what once comprised the noblest group of buildings in the province.

Elsewhere, on an Indian reserve rarely visited by the white traveler, another spired church enjoys a much more active life. Villagers worship there regularly and frequent it for community events. Consequently, they have cared for it far more attentively. A new concrete foundation keeps out the damp, modern doors and steps greet the worshipper, linoleum protects the floor, plywood paneling brightens the interior, and a suspended ceiling retains the heat.

Neither church, of course, is the building it once was. Formerly the most salient symbol of a new and vigorous way of life, and an architectural monument of beauty and significance, the Indian church has changed with the times. Indeed, to some people the church may seem little more than a conservation problem.

John Veillette and Gary White appreciated the many values of these outstanding buildings, and their dogged pursuit of dozens of Indian churches across the province has produced this handsome and important volume. In the past we may have realized that there was a fine tradition of mission church building in British Columbia; we had seen photographs of the destroyed churches at Sechelt and Metlakatla and had read about the work of Father A. G. Morice and the Reverend William Duncan, but never before had an extensive collection of pictures of extant (as well as lost) Indian churches been made available for enjoyment and study. Now, between the covers of a single book, we can at last absorb the fruits of a half-century of Indian church building from Vancouver Island to the Skeena Valley. No longer will the term "mission church" arouse visions only of the white adobe Franciscan buildings of California. For the first time, the wooden Indian churches of British Columbia can take their rightful place among the great specimens of North American architecture and culture.

At the beginning of the nineteenth century there were probably close to 100,000 native people living in what is now British Columbia. Their cultures, as Robin Fisher points out in his informative introductory essay, were among the richest and most vigorous on the continent. The social structures and rituals, particularly along the coast, were elaborate and opulent. But these cultures were not to continue without change. First came the fur traders, then the miners, the settlers, and the missionaries. Each wave of European contact contributed towards altering every aspect of the traditional Indian way of life.

As the natives adopted Christianity in ever increasing numbers, churches sprang up everywhere. Each village — and, as modern settlement patterns evolved, each reserve — built its own church. The mission church was more than a shelter for community worship. The missionaries must have envisaged them as potent symbols of Christian triumph, and thus in the more important villages both size and quality became essential features. (In areas where the denominations worked side by side, the drive for impressiveness may have been further inspired by sectarian rivalries.)

Despite a sophisticated native architectural tradition, the structures of the new churches were those of the newly arrived whites. An imposed culture was conveyed by an imposed architectural form. Builders ignored the traditional massive interlocking timber frame and the vertical boards of the Haida house, as they did the shed roof and the independently supported, horizontally planked wall of the Coast Salish house. In their place rose the horizontal logs and the clapboarded balloon frames of the pioneers. Architectural styles likewise reflected frontier fashion. The mission churches conformed to the nineteenth-century penchant for reviving earlier European modes of design. As Warren Sommer shows in his fascinating essay, the Gothic Revival played a particularly important role in the design and decoration of British Columbia churches, just as it had in every other corner of our continent.

One question that has always nagged visitors to Indian churches — and a problem linked to the denial of Indian building traditions — is *who* actually built them. In some cases the authors have succeeded in answering this key question. Many churches were apparently designed and executed by whites, and these, as might be expected, appear to have been by far the most elaborate. Belgian-born architect Joseph Bouillon and his Vancouver craftsmen designed and built the great mission church of Our Lady of the Rosary at Sechelt, resplendent in its twin bulbous-roofed and spired towers, traceried windows, and multiple buttresses. The single-towered church at Cranbrook, likewise professionally designed and built, also displays a design rich in architectural detail. The rigorously Gothic Revival second church at Hesquiat was built to the designs of Victoria architect Stephen Donovan by a pair of French-Canadian carpenters.

Native-built churches were notably simpler. At Canoe Creek, Oblate-educated Jimmy Brown, part Indian and part white, erected a plain gabled rectangular building with a stubby belfry. Its sawtoothed fretwork is charming but naive. The church at the Kamloops Reserve, built by a white carpenter who was assisted by Indian labour, was somewhat similar in quality although it sported a taller tower. Future research, perhaps exploiting the resources of oral history, may tell whether any churches were designed and built solely by Indian labour. At this stage it would be folly to speculate on the appearance of such buildings.

It may come as a surprise that no significant differences emerge between the churches of the missions and those in pioneer settlements. More recognizable distinctions may be found instead among the churches of the various denominations, whether built for natives or for whites. Roman Catholics (particularly Oblates) often built vertically and emulated — however many times removed — the great French cathedrals. Anglicans revived a different Gothic, that of the humbler and more picturesque English parish churches.

Often, however, the forms were so simplified by frontier forces as to blur any differences. Other denominations might shun the Gothic Revival, as did the Methodist missionaries of Greenville, who flirted instead with Georgian forms.

The regional variations described by the authors are attributable to local requirements, resources, and craft traditions, as Sommer explains, as well as to the pattern of prototype-and-imitation familiar to architectural historians. The pervasive image of the twin-towered church of Our Lady of the Rosary at Sechelt, for example, likely influenced not only the designs of the Indian churches at the North Vancouver and Musqueam reserves, but also that of the church (later cathedral) built ten years later in downtown Vancouver. In it the wood of the Indian churches has been translated into more permanent stone — the material of the original European sources — for a more affluent white urban congregation. The authors relate how Indians and missionaries from afar traveled to witness the consecration of the Sechelt masterpiece. They could only have been impressed. And so the churches at distant Bonaparte and Fountain emerged with spires of similar design, although both significantly feature the much simpler massing and detail characteristic of churches along the Lillooet-Brigade Trail.

Similarities within a region might even cross denominational lines. Thus the delightful little Anglican church at Pokhaist and the somewhat larger Catholic one at Shulus, both located in the Thompson-Nicola region, are composed and treated in the same manner.

Changing demographic and social patterns have conspired to leave many mission churches underused or unused. Hence so many stand in poor physical condition. Nobody, however, agrees as to whose problem the churches may be, nor even how the problem may be approached.

Are the churches the responsibility of the native people or of the religious orders and missionary societies that built them? Is it viable — or even just — to spend money restoring underutilized churches when the basic needs of so many natives in British Columbia remain unmet? If renovation be done, is change to be shunned today, whereas it is praised for having occurred in the past? The magnificent spire and handsome siding of Our Lady of Good Hope at Necoslie, for instance, were products of a 1905 modernization of an 1873 log church; those features were added in the same spirit in 1905 as plywood and concrete are used today.

If, indeed, a church becomes redundant, should it perhaps be used as a storage shed (as is the church at Nyshikup) or left derelict (as a reminder of our own time), or even be permitted to disappear with dignity? If a church be restored, should it be used for worship, as a community facility, or sold to private interests?

Conservation is no simple issue. It is one thing for a troubled observer to shout "Save it!" and another to find a solution that is both appropriate and feasible. Church redundancy has been debated in Britain and the United States, and public aid to church conservation is being considered in Ontario, but the situations there are not akin to that of the Indian churches of British Columbia. Perhaps the most constructive approach is that taken by Veillette and White themselves. Upset by the condition of the churches at Kitwanga and Glen Vowell, they took matters into their own hands. At the invitation of the local minister and band manager respectively, and with the assistance of villagers, they exchanged their cameras and clipboards for carpenters' tools and set to work repainting the deteriorated buildings. They relate these touching stories in a concluding essay.

Symbols of a past way of life, significant architectural monuments, and conservation problems — the early Indian village churches of British Columbia are all this and more. John Veillette and Gary White show a deep sensitivity for the objects of their study and their affection, and as a result this fine book will stand as a lasting record of a vanishing species.

HAROLD KALMAN

Preface

While majoring in Fine Arts at the University of British Columbia during the late 1960s, I found myself looking at pictures of pictures of pictures and listening to my friends plan trips to Europe to see the real thing. With courses in North American architecture behind me, however, I began to wonder if there were anything of historical and artistic importance closer to home that was neglected and worth recording. It was not long before I recalled the old wooden churches in Indian villages near Savona, B.C., where I had grown up. The fine church at Bonaparte, in particular, had always impressed me.

At this stage, my interest was vague and undirected, but in 1971 I met Gary White. During his years as manager and editor of the *Interior News* in Smithers, B.C., Gary had become strongly aware of the need to record local history, but his professional commitments afforded him no opportunity to carry out such a task. At the same time, his newspaper work had given him considerable experience with photography, while in contrast, until we met, my idea of a camera had been limited to the simplest of automatics. When he described the basic lack of historical data about the region served by the *Interior News*, it became apparent that we could combine our different kinds of expertise and experience to undertake some genuinely useful historical project.

During the following year, while I was employed at the Museum of Anthropology at the University of British Columbia, Gary and I made a trip to the Hazelton area of the Upper Skeena. The incredible richness of the region's culture was a revelation. It formed a great contrast to the austerity of the churches of the southern Interior and gave us the idea of a province-wide photographic inventory of early churches.

Research at the Provincial Archives and Museum and enquiries to the National Museum in Ottawa revealed the lack of any comprehensive record of early Indian mission churches. While there is a fairly rich photographic record of the coast villages, practically none exists of the early Interior settlements. In addition, it became apparent that the early traveling anthropologists and photographers had devoted most of their attention to the totem poles and the people and that they had overlooked the village churches almost completely.

At that point, we quit our jobs and, consolidating our resources, equipped ourselves with mobile living quarters containing darkroom facilities, cameras, and the other tools and trappings necessary to undertake the fieldwork that was to occupy us for the greater part of 1973 and 1974. This work in the field was the most interesting and enjoyable part of our project. As we moved from village to village in the province, we made many friendships that remain yet, and many people expressed their interest. But it was the old people who seemed the most pleased that the work was being done. Meeting with and talking to these old people have been among our richest experiences.

Financially we were hard-pressed and frequently ceased fieldwork to take employment of various kinds to fund the project. The assistance we received from several quarters, while deeply appreciated, was not substantial, and as a result the entire fieldwork phase was conducted on a shoestring budget. We were eventually able to cover nearly the entire province, but, while we make no excuses, our inadequate funding will explain to the reader why we were unable to visit some areas accessible only by boat or plane. Once our fieldwork was complete, we spent endless evenings printing the negatives in our darkroom and researching the history of the churches in archives and libraries.

As originally conceived, our project was to include all early churches, but during the course of fieldwork it became evident that of all the early churches in the province it is those in Indian villages that have remained the nearest to their original condition. Where early churches in non-Indian communities survive, they have frequently been so drastically remodeled or renovated that it is impossible to describe them as "early" in any meaningful sense. Today, however, it is the turn of the Indian church. A great deal of construction is taking place in the Indian villages, and the cost and difficulty involved in maintaining an old building make the future of the existing churches especially insecure. It was for these reasons that we chose to focus on the Indian village churches for this book. Although some interesting buildings have already been lost without being photographed, enough remain and enough are recorded in archival photographs to give a broad picture of the early churches in Indian villages and, in a sense, of all wooden frontier churches in British Columbia. This book has been built around these photographs; we took several thousand, mostly with 35 mm. cameras, but some with a 4″ x 5″ view camera.

We have divided the book into three main sections. In the first, Robin Fisher and Warren Sommer describe the historical background against which the Indian village churches were built. Robin Fisher discusses the dramatic growth of missionary activity among the Indians of British Columbia between 1850 and 1900; Warren Sommer explains how the churches were built and how technology and architectural traditions influenced their styles. Gary White and I then briefly describe Indian village life today and the state of the typical Indian village church.

In order to create manageable and meaningful groups of buildings in the second, and major, section of the book, we have organized the churches according to their location in eight geographical regions of the province. The coast is covered first, then the Interior, both of them from south to north. Within each regional group, we deal with the individual churches in an order that generally runs from west to east. To some extent, the grouping and ordering are arbitrary, but neither enthnographic nor denominational divisions seemed as useful as the geographical ones for presenting the individual churches in an orderly visual sequence.

Our third, very brief, section contains an account of the maintenance, restoration, and reconstruction work that Gary and I carried out on the Anglican church at Kitwanga and the Salvation Army hall at Glen Vowell.

Buildings covered in this volume range from tiny, rough churches to large, polished, and elegant examples. The number of buildings shown is limited for reasons of space, and the book does not include every existing early church, much less every one that has existed. We carefully chose our examples to give a representative picture of early village churches, and the particular photographs of each building were selected to emphasize the points I wished to make about the church. The treatment afforded each building inevitably reflects, in other words, my personal taste and is not intended to imply any judgment of relative importance. Our selection of churches is not meant to endorse one religious group or another, and no bias or slight is meant. I hope no offence will be taken. No buildings constructed after 1950 have been included.

We have deliberately not retouched archival photographs, with the single exception of the one showing the church at Fountain. In this case, we had access to a better photograph, which was unavailable for publication but which served as a reference.

Decisions regarding place names have been extremely difficult to make because several different spellings and even different names for the same village sometimes exist, but we have adopted local usage as the determining factor wherever a question arose. When villages are known by Indian names, Wilson Duff's book *The Indian History of British Columbia* and the 1916 Reserve Commission Report have been used as the authorities for the spelling of names not in the Gazetteer of Canada.

Most dates given are the dates of blessing or dedication ceremonies, which usually took place shortly after the completion of a building. It is these dates which parish records usually contain. In some cases, however, we are able to give the year of construction. In either case, when uncertainty exists, the date we offer is accurate, to the best of our knowledge, to within five years. In a few cases no information was available, and no date is given.

Our hope is that the book will bring these buildings to public attention and, particularly, to the attention of groups concerned with the preservation of our cultural heritage. It would be a tragedy indeed if, through neglect of this group of buildings, this volume were to become their only record. In addition, we hope that the book will create a new awareness and appreciation in those people who live in the villages served by these churches, that they will realize the importance of these buildings' contribution to the richness of our architectural heritage.

JOHN VEILLETTE

Acknowledgments

Throughout the fieldwork and preparation of the manuscript there have been many people who have kindly helped. We are grateful to all the people and organizations involved even if they are not mentioned specifically.

At the outset of the project financial help was given by The B.C. Conference of The United Church of Canada, B.C. Packers, Richmond Plywood, Mrs. Gordon T. Southam, St. Peter's Church, Hazelton, St. Hilda's Church, Savona, Mrs. McDowell, Mr. and Mrs. Harry Kruisselbrink, Mrs. Emile Veillette, Mrs. James Allan, and Mr. Wayne Worthington. Later, a grant from The Canada Council, Explorations Program, made it possible to organize the fieldnotes and print the negatives.

Early in the project the late Kay Cronin, author of *Cross in the Wilderness*, gave much encouragement and provided many helpful contacts in the field. Miss Helen Dawe has provided much information regarding the churches at Sechelt.

Mr. and Mrs. Norman Veillette and Mr. Jim Veillette of Savona helped a great deal with the fieldwork through the loan of vehicles and by their interest and encouragement.

We owe much to the many clergymen and others who helped by providing accommodation in their homes, suggesting churches we might otherwise miss, providing access to buildings, and answering questions, both in person and by mail. Father Lobsinger OMI, Father Black OMI, Rev. John Blyth, Rev. David Retter, Bishop Hambidge, Miss Eileen James, Rev. Robert Warren and his wife Solveig, Rev. Hubert McMillan, Father Haggerty OMI, Father Tom Lascelles OMI, Father Barry Desmond, Father Maglio, Father Van Leevwen, and Rev. Adams all deserve thanks.

During the last stages of the manuscript preparation, both Canon Cyril Williams of the Anglican Provincial Synod of B.C. and Mrs. Marilyn Harrison, the United Church archivist, helped solve some problems. Rev. Eric Powell of Christ Church Cathedral, Vancouver, provided help and encouragement throughout the project. Father Gaston Carrière OMI of the Archives Deschâtelets, Ottawa, has been most helpful, as has Father Martin Pollard SSB of Mount Angel Abbey, Oregon.

Others to whom we give special thanks include Mr. and Mrs. Isagani de Leon, the French family, Joseph and Josephine Bobby, Mr. Hank Thevarge, Mr. Ed Bennett, the late Mr. Charlie Draney, Mr. Sebastian Peters, Mr. and Mrs. Tommy Adolph, Mr. Cecil Russell, Mr. Peter Alfred, Mr. Alfred George, Mr. Joe Alec, Mr. Francis Edwards and his son Bill, Mrs. Louise Gabriel, Mr. Oliver Wilson, Mr. Walter Paul and his brother Terry, Mr. Anthony Joe, Mr. and Mrs. Ron Seymour, Mr. Auguste Mattis and Mr. Eugene Joseph, Mr. and Mrs. Guerin, and Mr. Cedric Sam. We also acknowledge the help of Mr. and Mrs. Jack Armstrong, who provided information about the Enderby church, and of Mr. Nuccio Spitali at Cranbrook.

We are grateful to the *Interior News* of Smithers, B.C., to Keith Marshall, the editor, and Dave Forsyth, photographer. Thanks, too, for much encouragement and helpful criticism from Mr. Eric Bunnell and last minute assistance, usually at a moment's notice, from Mrs. Jeanette Cuthbert.

We appreciate the efforts of the staff of the Ethnology Division of the Provincial Museum, especially Peter MacNair, Dan Savard, Elizabeth Virolainen, and Tim Paul. Thanks also for help with our own photographs to Mr. Rod Crowe, Mr. Andrew Niemann, Mr. Ray Bethell, and Mr. Rennie Knowlton.

The cooperation of the staff at the Provincial Archives was consistently given, for which we are indebted, and during the earlier years of the project, the help of Mr. Willard Ireland was most valuable.

We are grateful to Harold Kalman, Robin Fisher, and Warren Sommer for their written contributions to the book. Their enthusiasm and interest in the subject have helped to round out the book and make it more informative and valuable. It was partially as a result of Dr. Kalman's lectures on North American architecture at the University of British Columbia that this book was conceived.

Finally, special thanks are due to our many friends in Hazelton, to the people of Kitwanga and the people of Glen Vowell. By inviting us to live in their villages, all of these people have given us a rich experience and a better understanding of village life.

Major Ethnic Divisions of British Columbia Indians

Missions to the Indians of British Columbia

ROBIN FISHER

Effective missionary work among the Indians of British Columbia did not begin until the middle of the nineteenth century, and yet the early missionaries apparently met with rapid and remarkable success. By the beginning of the twentieth century virtually all of the Indians were sufficiently convinced by missionary teaching to declare themselves Christian. Many factors explain this Indian response to Christianity. The nature of the traditional Indian cultures, the consequences of contact between the Indians and the European fur-traders and settlers, the background and objectives of the missionaries, and the techniques that they used in British Columbia all had a bearing on the Indian reaction to the missionaries and their message.

Haida carving

THE TRADITIONAL INDIAN CULTURES

By the time of the coming of the European, the Indians of the area that was to become British Columbia had, over many centuries, developed cultural patterns of great richness and diversity. On the coast, where the population was concentrated, the Indian cultures were among the most vigorous and elaborate in North America. The boundaries of these cultures may be defined along linguistic lines, and the accompanying map shows the variety of Indian languages in the region. There were at least twenty-four mutually exclusive languages, representing seven of the eleven major Indian language families in Canada.

The great cultural diversity makes generalizations about the Indians both difficult and dubious. Even though the northwest coast, for instance, is often seen as a single culture area, the common patterns should not obscure the important variations between the groups. On the northern coast, the cultures of the Haida and the Tsimshian were similar but not the same, and there were considerable differences between the Haida and the Coast Salish to the south. Both the Haida and the Tsimshian had very clearly defined social structures and matrilineal kinship systems. In both societies the local group was divided into clans, whose members were only permitted to marry men or women belonging to another one; but Haida villages were split into two clans — Eagle and Raven — while Tsimshian groups had three or even four — Eagle, Raven, Wolf, and Killer Whale. Similarly, Haida and Tsimshian art shared common characteristics, but the bold austerity of the figures on Haida totem poles contrasted sharply with the crowded, fussy groupings on many Tsimshian poles. Among the Coast Salish, social divisions were not so clearly defined as they were in the northern groups. Kinship tended to be determined patrilineally, and clans did not exist. Coast Salish art, too, was

Tsimshian carving

Coast Salish carved house post

quite different. In the eyes of many European beholders, it was also less impressive than Haida art.

There was a fundamental division between the Indians of the coast and those who lived inland. On the coast the Indians lived in an abundant maritime environment and had evolved a complex social structure, elaborate and opulent ceremonies, and a highly stylized art form. East of the coastal mountains the natural environment was less prolific, and in order to gather the resources of the land, the Indians had to be more mobile. Partly as a consequence of this mobility, the social organization of the Interior Indians was looser, and, in comparison with the coast Indians, their ritual and material culture appeared less elaborate.

Given this basic division between the coast and the Interior, there was also great cultural variety among the inland groups. Those Interior Indians who were in contact with the coast absorbed some features of the coastal cultures. The Chilcotin, for example, had a version of the potlatch ceremony typical of the coastal groups. In the southeast, many aspects of the Kootenay Indian culture were similar to features of the culture of the plains Indians, whom they contacted during the annual buffalo hunt east of the Rockies.

While there was great cultural variety, there were a number of aspects of the traditional Indian way of life that probably assisted the work of the missionaries. Christian missionaries in other parts of the world found it difficult to work among indigenous peoples who were constantly on the move. Frequently, they attempted to convince nomadic groups to adopt a settled, preferably agricultural, way of life. But this change in lifestyle was not quite so necessary among the Indians of the northwest coast of British Columbia. During the summer the larger groups split up into smaller units that scattered to the various food-gathering locations, but they always spent the winter in the large plank houses of the permanent villages, where the missionaries could work with them at one place. With summer over and the material needs of man attended to, the winter was traditionally the period for exploring and celebrating the spiritual aspects of life. It was the time for winter dancing and for potlatching — the ritual in which the Indians gave property away to establish their prestige and position. Much of the dancing and ceremony that frequently accompanied these rituals was designed to propitiate mythical figures. The missionaries later objected strenuously to most of these practices, but the ritual and ceremony were those of a people accustomed to exploring the spiritual dimension; ultimately, Indian spirituality was not entirely incompatible with Christianity. The Indians paid homage to spiritual and mythical beings who were then expected to work for man, to protect him and help provide for his needs. If the Indians decided to accept the Christian God and he proved effective, his name could simply be added to those of their existing deities.

Within most Indian cultures the connection between the spiritual and the material worlds was represented by the shaman, a man who fulfilled the functions of both doctor and priest and called on the assistance of the spirits to cure physical maladies. Because their roles were so similar, the shaman and the missionary came into instant conflict; but because the Indians were familiar with the function of the shaman, they could readily appreciate the intentions of the missionaries. Similarly, the presence of strong leaders in their own societies meant that the Indians were accustomed to the kind of role that the missionaries would attempt to assume. Although Indian chiefs led through prestige and influence rather than power and authority, Indian societies in British Columbia were definitely hierarchical, and leadership was well developed. Many missionaries had strong and forceful personalities, and they tended to usurp traditional leadership roles at the same time as they built upon them. Sometimes the conversion of an Indian leader could influence the decision of Indians of lower rank.

CONSEQUENCES OF EUROPEAN CONTACT

During the fur-trading period from the 1780s to the 1850s acculturative forces changed and modified but did not disrupt the Indian cultures. The fur trade itself introduced new wealth that stimulated a flowering of art and ceremony without upsetting basic cultural patterns. In fact, some Indian groups — or perhaps more accurately, some Indian leaders — were able to exercise a great deal of control over the fur trade. They became very wealthy and, in a society where the two were closely related, also very powerful. But while disparities in wealth and power may have increased, the Indians remained in control of their own situation. One other effect of contact in the fur-trading period had a bearing on later developments. As the Indians moved to be closer to the centres of trade, larger concentrations of population sometimes developed. And it was often among groups of Indians who had established themselves near a trading post like Fort Simpson that the missionaries began their work.

By the late 1850s, when the missionaries began arriving in appreciable numbers, the fur trade was passing, and the Indians were being affected by the disruptive pressures of the settlement frontier. Gold miners and settlers who came to British Columbia began to utilize the resources of land, sea, and river increasingly to the exclusion of the Indians. As a consequence the pace of cultural change among the Indians increased rapidly. After the mainland colony was established in 1858, government land policy invariably reflected the views of the settlers, and it had the effect of confining the Indians on smaller and smaller reserves. These were often too small to produce a livelihood, and some Indians moved to the towns in order to benefit from the economic opportunities that they offered. But while they were cutting their ties with the old culture Indians were not made welcome by the new. Drunkenness and disease, particularly, were associated with the towns, and these evils concerned Indian elders who worried about the erosion of the traditional cultures. It was with this environment that the missionaries began to be effective. Indeed, some historians of Christian missions to indigenous peoples have argued that a degree of cultural disruption is a prerequisite for missionary success; only in a situation where old ways and values are proving ineffective or are being called into question will new ones be considered.

THE MISSIONARIES AND THEIR BACKGROUND

The missionaries who came to British Columbia arrived conscious of their personal limitations but with a prodigious confidence in the power of their

God, in the efficacy of their religion, and in the superiority of their culture. They were not just the representatives of mid-nineteenth-century Christianity but also of western European culture; and they came with the firm intention of effecting social as well as religious change among the Indians.

They came largely as a result of developments of religious thought in Europe. The nineteenth century saw a new surge of interest in missions in the Roman Catholic Church. Old orders were reorganized and again assumed a missionary role, and new orders especially devoted to missionary work were founded. Among these new orders was the Congregation of Missionary Oblates of Mary Immaculate, which was established in 1826 by Eugène de Mazenod. It became the major Roman Catholic missionary order in British Columbia. The Protestant missionaries espoused a form of Christianity that was the product of a spiritual revolution in the late eighteenth century. This revolution had given birth not only to Methodism but also to an evangelical movement within the Anglican church. In the late 1850s a resurgence of this evangelical movement led to the formation of new missionary societies, while older ones like the Anglican Church Missionary Society (CMS) attracted increased support and a growing number of recruits. These recruits were often men and women whose first conversion to an intensely felt form of Christianity was followed by a second conversion to the missionary vocation. A vivid realization of personal sinfulness led to a desire to be, in John Wesley's words, *Born again of the spirit*. This experience of personal rebirth led to a desire to be instrumental in the salvation of others, to be obedient to the biblical injunction to *preach the gospel to every creature*, and particularly to save the *perishing heathen* from Satan's grasp.

The missionaries saw this task as a great opportunity. According to them, man without God was utterly evil, and only their efforts could save the unconverted from eternal damnation. As one who came to British Columbia asked rhetorically, *What joy can be equal to this? To have a part in the deliverance of whole nations from the power of Satan, and from ignorance, to the knowledge of the true God*. They believed that all men were equal, since before God all souls were equal; to have believed otherwise would have been to invalidate their vocation. But at the same time, they also believed that only through their work could the potential equality of native peoples become a real equality.

While this deeply and sincerely felt religious motivation was paramount, other factors also drove these individuals to labour in isolated parts of the world among peoples whose way of life was so different from their own. Many were men of humble birth who had struggled to rise above their origins. For some the decision to work as a missionary was an extension of their drive for success in the secular world. As missionaries in foreign lands they could achieve the social respectability and positions of leadership that they had striven for at home. In addition, missionary candidates were often men of great energy and force who hoped to find in the mission field a freedom of action and a scope for their enterprise that was denied them in Europe. Some were impelled by a simple desire to live in an exotic land, or by the same love of adventure that sent explorers to far away places.

THE MISSIONARIES IN BRITISH COLUMBIA

Franciscan friars accompanied the first Spanish explorers to the northwest coast of North America, but their confident expectation that large numbers would immediately accept their teachings was not realized. When the Hudson's Bay Company developed its operations west of the Rockies in the first half of the nineteenth century, Roman Catholic missionaries sometimes traveled with the fur brigades north from Fort Vancouver on the Columbia River. In some places these men baptized large numbers of Indians, but few of them were genuinely converted. In 1829, the first Protestant missionary, the Reverend Jonathan Green, came to the area and visited several locations on the northwest coast. His advice that a mission should be established in the area was apparently ignored by the society which he represented, the American Board of Commissioners for Foreign Missions. Even the missionaries conceded that these first contacts with the Indians were superficial. It was not until the late 1850s that missionary work was intensified and became organized enough to produce real results.

Roman Catholic priests worked on Vancouver Island following its establishment as a British colony in 1849. Then, in 1858, the Oblates of Mary Immaculate established a centre for their operations at Esquimalt, and in the same year the Sisters of Saint Ann arrived in Victoria to begin their work. In the previous year William Duncan had arrived, the first and the most famous of the Church Missionary Society's representatives to come to British Columbia. And in 1859, the Society for the Propagation of the Gospel in Foreign Parts, another Church of England agency, sent its first missionaries to the area. Also in 1859, Methodist missionaries from Upper Canada arrived to begin their work on the west coast.

During the 1860s and 1870s the missionaries extended their operations to include most of the Indian groups of the coast and the southern Interior. In October 1857, Duncan left Victoria and moved to Fort Simpson to begin preaching and teaching among the Tsimshian. Five years later, he took a group of his followers and established the model village at Metlakatla. Like many missionaries, Duncan was egocentric and obdurate, personality traits which were intensified by living for long periods in relative isolation among an alien people. He refused to accept ordination and to administer the sacrament of Holy Communion to his Tsimshian villagers, and, when the Reverend William Ridley was appointed over him as the first bishop of Caledonia, he refused to accept episcopal authority. In 1887 as a result of this conflict he moved to Annette Island in Alaska and founded New Metlakatla.

In spite of personality differences, other missionaries worked with Duncan at Metlakatla before moving off to establish their own missions among the Tsimshian. At Kincolith on the Nass River, the Reverend Robert Tomlinson founded a missionary village. He modeled the settlement on Metlakatla, as did the Reverend J. B. McCullagh at Aiyansh in 1883. Work began among the Queen Charlotte Haida when the Reverend W. H. Collison established the Massett mission in 1878, and two years later a CMS mission to the Kwakiutl was started. Other Anglicans, under the auspices of the Society for the Propagation of the Gospel, began missions on both Vancouver Island and the lower mainland.

William Duncan

Thomas Crosby

During the first twenty years of their work in British Columbia, the Methodists concentrated their forces on the lower mainland and the northern coast. The first of them limited their impact on the Indians by ministering to the European and the native populations at the same time. It was Thomas Crosby who developed the Methodist Indian mission as a separate entity. Arriving in 1862, Crosby was both young and enthusiastic. He began his work at Nanaimo, later moved to Chilliwack, and in 1873 established a mission at Port Simpson. Crosby's work there led to the establishment of a substantial permanent village which in many ways rivaled Metlakatla.

Moving out from their centre in Esquimalt, the Oblates greatly extended the area of their influence in the 1860s. The first mainland station had been established in 1859 when Father Charles Pandosy began work among the Okanagan Indians. Other stations were founded in the Interior at Kamloops and Williams Lake, but it was in the lower Fraser Valley that Roman Catholic influence was strongest. In 1861 Father Leon Forquet began Saint Mary's mission near the present site of Mission City, and it soon became a major centre of missionary work among the Salish.

Particularly in the Sechelt area, the Oblates developed a system of model villages so that they could more effectively control practically every aspect of the lives of their converts. The success of these villages can be measured partly by the fact that in 1871 the missionaries administered the sacrament of confirmation to all of the Sechelt Indians. The Oblates were also active on Vancouver Island, although they had their most notable failure among the resolute Kwakiutl of Fort Rupert. This mission was eventually abandoned because the Indians showed no sign at that time of giving up their traditional beliefs and accepting those of Christianity.

In the last two decades of the nineteenth century, denominations already working in British Columbia sent missionaries into new areas until they covered nearly all of the province. Both the Anglicans and the Methodists moved up the Skeena River to minister to the Gitksan of the Hazelton area. The Roman Catholics also extended their influence northwards. In 1880 Father A. G. Morice arrived in British Columbia and was sent to Williams Lake. He moved to Fort Saint James in 1885, and for nearly twenty years he was the dominant missionary personality in the northern Interior. In addition to becoming widely respected for his missionary work, Morice also became well known for his extensive and diverse writing on the development of the Roman Catholic Church in western Canada, the history of northern British Columbia, and the culture and language of the Carrier Indians.

In the two decades between 1880 and 1900, new denominations became active. Among the Tsimshian groups, the Salvation Army met with some success and in 1898 set up a village at Glen Vowell near the Indian village of Kispiox. The Presbyterian Church, too, began work, particularly among the Nootka on the west coast of Vancouver Island.

Where denominational spheres of influence coincided or overlapped rivalry sometimes led to conflict. Some missionaries even seemed to expend more of their energy fighting the influence of other denominations than converting the Indians. Hostility, particularly between Protestants and Roman Catholics, was not uncommon. The Church Missionary Society held that *Romanised heathenism* was far more difficult to deal with than the original form, and the Methodist missionary John Robson claimed that the Roman Catholics only effected superficial change among the Indians when they baptized them and taught them the sign of the cross without demanding any fundamental alteration of lifestyle. Eventually, however, accommodations had to be reached, and the present distribution of Indian churches corresponds to separate areas of denominational influence.

MISSIONARY OBJECTIVES

There can be no doubt that the missionaries of all the denominations, particularly in the early years, were aggressive agents of change, both spiritual and secular, among the Indians of British Columbia. According to the Reverend George Hills, the first bishop of Columbia, the missionary laboured to inculcate a new set of religious beliefs that would cleanse the Indians *from the awful superstitions in which they were ... sunk.* The missionaries demanded that their converts experience an inner change of values and that they totally eradicate their indigenous religious beliefs and replace them with the tenets of mid-nineteenth-century Christianity. With their vivid understanding of sin and its consequences in hell, the missionaries perceived this form of spiritual conversion as an urgent matter. But they required even more than spiritual change of their Indian converts. Along with an inner conversion to the new religion, thoroughgoing outward changes in behaviour were called for, so that the Christian Indian would become a completely new being in every way. The missionaries saw this temporal facet of their work as no less pressing than their spiritual responsibilities.

A. G. Morice

William Duncan asserted in his first report from British Columbia that *civilization apart from Christianity has no vitality*; but he, and indeed most missionaries, also believed that the reverse was equally true. Accordingly, an attack on the social practices of the Indians was to accompany the conversion of the heathen. As Tomlinson put it, the objective of the CMS missionaries was not only *to overthrow dark spiritualism and plant instead Christian truth* but also to *change the natives from ignorant bloodthirsty cruel savages into quiet useful subjects of our Gracious Queen.* The Roman Catholics likewise demanded great social reformation, although, possibly as a result of centuries of missionary experience, they were slightly less dogmatic about it than the Protestants.

There were many aspects of the traditional Indian cultures that the missionaries objected to and therefore, particularly in the early years, sought to change. At Lytton the Reverend J. B. Good began his mission by pointing out to the Indians, who had requested his presence, *all their manifold hypocrisy, uncleanness, and idleness, and many other sins and evil practices.* The potlatch ritual was essential to the culture of the coast Indians, but the missionaries saw it as *foolish, wasteful and demoralizing* and perhaps the most formidable obstacle in the way of their work. It was largely as a result of missionary pressure that the Federal Government declared the ceremony illegal in the 1884 amendment to the Indian Act. Although the potlatch is probably the best known example, it was only one of the many Indian practices that the missionaries tried to eradicate. When Thomas Crosby was at Nanaimo, the Indians asked him if they could continue some of their tradi-

Turn-of-the-century potlatch, Alert Bay

7

tional customs as long as they also attended church and sent their children to school. But Crosby would not bend. He told the Indians that they must give up all the old ways: *the dance, the potlatch etc., it is all bad.* Such determination was typical of missionaries who wanted to teach the Indians that *Christianity meant nothing less than the subversion of every evil work and no compromise.*

MISSIONARY TECHNIQUES

Preaching and teaching were the most important techniques used by the missionaries to achieve change. The missionaries' first task when making contact with different groups of Indians was to begin to communicate the new ideas through sermons. To this end, many of them struggled to learn the Indian languages. Duncan had only been at Fort Simpson for a few months before he first preached to the Indians in Tsimshian. One can only imagine what garbled version of Christian theology he conveyed to the Indians under these circumstances. But the missionaries were certainly not satisfied with the fur traders' Chinook jargon, since they intended to have a much more fundamental and lasting influence on the minds of the Indians.

Mission schoolroom, Kitwanga

Through their schools, where they met their pupils on a day-to-day basis, the missionaries hoped to re-educate the young in particular. As the photographs of Saint Paul's at Kitwanga (p. 69) and the Methodist church at Port Simpson (p. 60) indicate, the school was the second most important building on the mission station, and instructing the Indians was an integral and important part of the work of most missionaries. Pupils were taught the basics of reading, writing, and arithmetic, as well as religious knowledge and some of the "useful arts" of western civilization. While they were often unsuccessful, the missionaries also made efforts to inculcate habits of "order, discipline, and cleanliness." Their methods of teaching were frequently those that had been developed in British Sunday schools. The monitorial system involved the older pupils instructing the younger ones by a question-and-answer method, and it was widely used, especially in the Protestant missions. It had two advantages for an isolated missionary: it required a limited amount of equipment; and a minimum number of teachers could instruct the maximum number of pupils. Its disadvantage was that it involved rote learning rather than "education" in the broadest sense of the word.

On a larger scale, missionaries commonly set about their work by establishing separate Christian villages. There they could isolate their followers from outside influences and exercise greater control over both potential and actual converts. Within the confines of these villages, the missionaries regulated nearly every aspect of the lives of their congregations. Lists of rules were drawn up, and Indians were appointed to police them. At the same time, some missionaries also established village industries to provide for the Indians' material needs. Frequently the lumber mills and workshops that the missionaries founded provided much of the woodwork for the village churches. The Church Missionary Society's showplace at Metlakatla was the most famous but by no means the only example of the tightly regulated missionary village designed to effect radical and wholesale adjustments in the Indians' way of life.

The churches that the missionaries directed the Indians to build provide a measure of the degree of cultural change they meant to achieve. The Indians, especially those of the northern coast, had developed a very powerful style of house building using the readily available cedar. But whether the churches were imposing structures like the ones at Metlakatla (p. 57) and Sechelt (p. 34) or rudimentary chapels like those at Shackan (p. 104) and Pinchi (p. 170), their style was European rather than Indian. While they were sometimes built of cedar, they included many features developed by European stone masons that were often unnecessarily ornate or even superfluous in wood constructions. At one time, the church at Metlakatla had a number of crude Tsimshian wooden sculptures in one of its side chapels, but this was the exception that proves the rule. In the main, the churches expressed the missionaries' overall intent to replace that which was Indian with that which was European.

Today it is fashionable to be critical of these early missionaries, because they were so aggressive in their efforts to modify Indian cultures. Apart from the fact that these criticisms often involve an ahistorical judgment, whereby nineteenth-century men are condemned for not behaving according to twentieth-century precepts, it is frequently forgotten that the Indians were experiencing severe cultural disruption in the second half of the nineteenth century as a result of other European contact. Indeed, so disturbing were the changes facing the Indians that many settlers in British Columbia thought that there was little point in making provision for them, since they were destined, sooner or later, to die out. The missionaries were more optimistic. They very definitely saw a future for the Indians, although it was a future seen in terms of the Indian closely imitating the European. For the missionaries, the possibility that the Indians might become extinct as a result of white contact only increased the urgency of their work. They thus took the humanitarian view that colonization need not be a complete disaster for the indigenous people, provided the right steps were taken rapidly to save the Indians from the worst effects of settlement.

Having taken this position, the missionaries often acted to protect the Indians from the most destructive consequences of the settlement frontier. They frequently, for example, acted as advocates for the Indians in their disagreements with the government over the land question. Many of the earliest petitions sent to the government of British Columbia were written by missionaries and expressed Indian grievances about land policy. In 1868 when a group of lower Fraser chiefs wrote to Governor Frederick Seymour complaining about the reduction of their reserves, they acted in consultation with Father Paul Durieu. Later, as bishop of New Westminster, Durieu supported their objections again in 1874, and in the same year, Father C. J. Grandidier wrote at length to the *Victoria Standard* describing Indian complaints over land in the Interior. The Roman Catholics were not alone in this kind of activity, for William Duncan, along with other Protestants, also objected to the government's treatment of the Indians and their land.

The missionaries, of course, had an ulterior interest in the land question. If the Indians became settled farmers, missionary work would be made easier. But the Indians could only settle if the government reserved sufficient good land for them. Ulterior motives aside, however, the missionaries were

Indian carvings in side-chapel at Metlakatla

correct in their view that the Indians had to have some viable economic activity as a base if they were to play a significant role in British Columbia society.

Apart from the issues involving Indian land, one of the social problems that most concerned the missionaries was alcohol. They wanted to keep their Indian followers away from the temptations of *ardent spirits* and therefore did their best to limit the illegal activities of whisky sellers. Even in the early years of settlement drunkenness had become a serious matter among those Indians who had access to liquor. Prostitution and its attendant disease were further less desirable aspects of European civilization from which the missionaries tried to protect the Indians.

Ironically, to the extent that they encouraged peaceful relations between Indians and Europeans, the missionaries also assisted the advance of the settlement frontier. But there was an important distinction between the missionaries and the settlers. The impact of the settlers on the Indians was largely destructive. Indian cultures were eroded and the settlers proposed nothing to take their place. The missionaries consciously tried to eradicate many Indian customs, but they also presented an alternative.

The notion that the missionaries brought only unmitigated destruction to the Indian cultures is perhaps as naive as that of earlier missionary apologists, who had nothing but praise for every missionary activity. Such a view also fails to recognize any resilience on the part of the Indians. During the first years of missionary work in British Columbia, the native population responded in a great many ways — ranging from absolute acceptance to total rejection — to the missionaries and their message.

INDIAN RESPONSES

It is clear that by the turn of the century, when the influence of the missionaries was probably at its peak, most of the Indians of British Columbia were at least nominally Christian. The census return in the annual report of the Department of Indian Affairs for 1900 indicates that of a total Indian population of 24,696 in the province, 19,504 called themselves Christian. Only 2,696 were enumerated as *pagan*, while the religion of another 2,900 was unknown. The Roman Catholic church had the largest number of Indian adherents with 11,846, and the Anglicans and Methodists were second and third with 4,210 and 3,068 respectively. The largest groups of Indians still holding traditional beliefs were on the coast, particularly among the Nootka and to a lesser extent among the Kwakiutl, Tsimshian, and Haida. By 1920 this pattern was little changed. Of a total Indian population of 25,694, 21,560 were recorded as being Christian. The proportions belonging to the three leading denominations were about the same, although fewer — 1,421 — were described as adhering to *aboriginal beliefs*.

Some of these converts undoubtedly observed only the form of the new religion. Contemporary sceptics often claimed that the Indians merely recited the liturgy of their church without making any great change in their way of life. Many were probably attracted to Christianity by the novelty of the ritual and the teaching. It has also been suggested that indigenous people who accept Christianity do so out of a desire for the material goods to which the missionaries provided access. In some cases this may have been the dominant motivation, yet there is no reason to assume that other Indians did not approach Christianity on the level of ideas and embrace it for theological reasons. There obviously were Indians who experienced a conversion that involved absolute changes in their beliefs and in their way of life. Certainly the missionaries, in their enthusiasm, considered that the power of God had been demonstrated by the *raising of a large body of people from the degradations of heathenism to the position of happy contented members of civilized society.*

Although their numbers were always decreasing, other Indians absolutely rejected Christianity. They dismissed the religious teaching of the missionaries or simply refused to give up as many of their traditional customs as the uncompromising missionaries demanded. Resistance was particularly strong from those who had a greater investment in the continuation of the old lifestyle. However, while older people and Indian leaders often rejected Christianity in the early years, it is not true that only slaves or people of low rank were converted. Among some groups resistance took the form of attempts to reassert traditional Indian culture in the face of the missionary inroads. Duncan at Metlakatla had to face at least one revolt led by a Tsimshian shaman supported by one of the traditional chiefs. Often the result of these tensions was to divide Indian communities into pro- and anti-missionary factions.

From the beginning of missionary work in British Columbia, the missionaries were dogmatic in their approach, but the Indians were flexible in their response. Christianity was thus absorbed by Indians who also retained many of the old beliefs and customs. Soon after the initial missionary contacts, "prophet" cults sprang up that were a mixture of Christian and Indian elements. Typically these movements were led by Indians who had been in contact with missionary teaching, and the Reverend Good recalled one such movement on the Fraser River in the 1870s. The Indian prophet and his followers looked forward to the day when the Europeans would be ejected from the area and all that they had taken would be restored to the Indians. Less anti-European and more permanent in its influence has been the Shaker church. Established in Washington State in the 1880s, this sect later moved to southern British Columbia where it still has some members.

While most Indians today are still at least nominally Christian, the increasing tendency has been for Christianity to become integrated within Indian cultures, so that among many groups there now exists an amalgam of Christian and traditional beliefs. Spirit dancing is still carried on, particularly among the Coast Salish, and winter dancing continues among other coastal groups. Even the shaman, whose activities were attacked so vigorously by the missionaries, still treats some illnesses. The missionaries were certainly both ethnocentric and intransigent in their denunciation of many Indian practices, but the Indian cultures did not suddenly collapse. The fact that many of the fine churches built by the missionaries are now derelict or in poor repair shows that they did not impose their will and their culture entirely. In the long run, the alien symbols have often been rejected or modified by Indians who have remained resistant to many of the pressures of acculturation.

Mission Church Architecture on the Industrial Frontier

WARREN SOMMER

CHURCH SITES

The distribution of British Columbia's Indian churches generally corresponds with the map of individual denominational strengths. Hence, Roman Catholic churches stand in the Interior, the lower coast, the lower Fraser Valley, and on parts of Vancouver Island. Anglican churches are found in the Skeena and Nass valleys, on the lower coast, in the territory around Lytton, and on Vancouver Island. Methodist ministers and congregations erected churches on the Queen Charlotte Islands, in the Skeena and Nass valleys, along the central coast, on Vancouver Island, and in the villages near Chilliwack. Church construction by Presbyterians was confined to the southwest part of Vancouver Island, while the Salvation Army built only in the Skeena and Nass river valleys.

Missionaries generally encouraged the construction of Indian churches wherever and whenever sympathetic congregations were sufficiently Christianized. In a few instances church construction actually preceded the first visit of the missionary, so anxious were the Indians to gain missionary favour and attention. In some villages churches were built only a few months after a missionary made his first contacts with the native inhabitants. Most churches, however, were built several years after initial contacts were made.

For the missionaries, church construction served two important purposes. First, churches were useful as places of instruction, prayer, and sacramental worship. Second, the building of churches strengthened a missionary's hold on the villages he had claimed. By directing his followers to construct a church a missionary informed rival denominations that he had the confidence and support of the natives and that interference would only be a waste of time and effort.

Missionaries, of course, had to be careful that they did not build before their doctrines were firmly established. In the mid-1860s the Methodists evangelized the Indians of Sroyalas near Chilliwack and had a church built there. The construction was premature, however, for by 1887 the Indians had become Roman Catholic, and the Methodist church stood empty and unused.

As a rule, missionaries delayed building churches until they were absolutely sure that their efforts would not be fruitless. Accordingly, many waited until the 1890s before they built. By then, most of the province's Indians were irrevocably allied with one or another particular sect, and denominational positions were relatively secure. Further, after about 1890 the Canadian government provided funds for education to denominations that built churches or schools in Indian villages. As a result, denominations working in particular villages gained a semi-official status.

Indian churches were normally built in or near traditional winter encampments or settlements. Since the construction of churches presented opportunities to create completely new Christian villages, however, exact locations were often decreed by missionaries. Most denominations followed a common procedure when establishing such new communities. Missionaries chose sites on the outskirts of "heathen" villages, directed that churches be built at the new locations, and then encouraged the Indians to build single-family houses around the churches.

In a few important cases, unusually large churches were built at quite some distance from traditional Indian encampments. Their construction usually followed the creation of model villages, when missionaries uprooted several Indian bands, moved them to central locations, and molded them into single social units. Most British Columbian model villages of this kind were Roman Catholic creations, although Duncan's Anglican settlement at Metlakatla was a notable Protestant example. In 1880 Father Morice described the North Vancouver model village created by the Oblate priests of New Westminster. [It] *consists of three rows of uniform, whitewashed houses. They aren't quite as comfortable as American houses, but for the Indians, they are the best for which one could hope. The church stands on a green lawn in the centre of the village, and dominates the houses. Every day, morning and evening, the Indians gather there for prayers and songs of praise.*

Attempts to create such settlements at Oblate central missions like St. Eugene and Mission were less successful: particularly large churches were built at most of these missions, but they were large in order to house periodic reunions or gatherings of bands living elsewhere. Since the Indians resisted resettlement, and the government failed to provide sufficient land for agriculture, the missionaries found the model-village projects extremely difficult to execute; they moderated their interest in moving the Indians and concentrated instead on "uplifting" them in their ancestral locations.

Early photograph of the Roman Catholic village of Hagwilget, showing the dominant position of the church

ARCHITECTURAL STYLE

British Columbia's mission churches were shaped by three principal forces: the liturgical and architectural traditions of each denomination, the individual tastes of clergymen, and the varying woodworking abilities of the province's Indians. Denominational traditions generally determined the floor plans and basic forms of churches, while missionaries and Indian builders added their own decorative detail. Since each denomination concentrated its buildings regionally, and since the skills of Indian carpenters and the tastes of individual missionaries varied from one part of the province to the next, regionally distinct styles of churches sometimes evolved. [The features of these styles are discussed in the photographic section of the book where each region of the province is introduced individually — Ed.]

In spite of regional and denominational differences, British Columbia's Indian churches owe much to the liturgical and architectural traditions of Europe and eastern Canada. In frontier conditions, where no local tradition of church architecture existed, traditions brought by missionaries from their homes asserted themselves. Anglican missionaries based their churches on prototypes in England. Methodists and Presbyterians modeled their churches on buildings they had known in Britain and eastern Canada. The Salvation Army patterned its buildings after chapels in England. And among the Roman Catholics there were two influences. The diocesan priests of Vancouver Island and the Sisters of St. Ann, a teaching order, drew from church designs in the province of Quebec. The Oblate priests of the mainland, however, based the designs of their churches on French and Belgian examples.

Because they were modeled on buildings in Europe and eastern Canada, British Columbia's early mission churches reflect the historical styles revived by late nineteenth-century European churchbuilders. By far the most important and influential of these styles in British Columbia was Gothic, characterized by its pointed arches and its generally vertical lines. The Gothic Revival emerged from the romanticism of late eighteenth- and early nineteenth-century Britain. The style was at first an architectural expression of escape; it was a rejection of the cold rationalism of Georgian architecture, which was based on Greek and Roman styles, and a partial withdrawal from the horrors of industrialization. Eighteenth-century poets and novelists began the movement by proclaiming the glories, beauties, and mysteries of mediaeval Britain. Interest in the art and architecture of the Middle Ages consequently grew first among the elite.

But public interest in England in the Gothic style increased dramatically when churchmen were swayed by the combined arguments of A. W. N. Pugin, the Oxford Tractarians, and the Cambridge Camden Society. A. Welby Pugin was a professional architect who first gained popular attention in 1836 when he published *Contrasts*. In this book he drew an impassioned comparison between the hideous and immoral cities and towns of the nineteenth century and the noble architecture and superior values of the Middle Ages. The Oxford Tractarians, named for their connections with Oxford University and their series of *Tracts for the Times*, were clergymen who looked back to the church of the seventeenth century, the Middle Ages, and beyond. They hoped to desecularize the Church of England and make it once again *a divine society and a sacred mystery*. The Camden Society was founded at Cambridge University in 1839. Its members linked the mysticism of the Tractarians with Pugin's mediaeval romanticism by maintaining that mediaeval builders had planned their churches with symbolic intent. The nave, for example, symbolized the earthly body of Christ, the Church Militant. The chancel represented the heavenly church, the Church Triumphant. And the division between the two, usually marked by a roodscreen or chancel arch, symbolized the Sacrifice of Christ. The Anglican Church, in particular, adopted rules of building style and arrangement that reflected this symbolism. It continued to obey them long after the interpretations of mediaeval builders' intentions on which the rules were based had been disproven or forgotten.

Virtually all Anglican mission churches in early British Columbia follow the Camden Society's broad guidelines. This fact is not surprising, for in the late nineteenth century, most of the province's Anglican missionaries were English. Many were educated at Oxford and Cambridge, the very universities that gave birth to serious Gothic revivalism. Others were trained at missionary colleges attached to great English cathedrals, and some were staunch Tractarians.

An Anglican mission church, therefore, generally consists of a nave and chancel, a belfry or tower, an entrance porch, and a vestry. The nave houses the congregation; the chancel houses the choir and clergy. Vestries accommodate clergymen on overnight visits and provide storage for vestments, communion wares, and other items used in services. Most mission churches follow an east-west axis with their chancels at the east and their naves and towers toward the west. Vestries are usually to one side of the chancel. Entry porches are commonly near the nave's southwestern corner, and, if they are included in the tower, they are usually at the nave's western end. Naves generally have single, central aisles, with pews and kneelers to either side. Wooden fonts are sometimes placed symbolically near the nave's western door to represent the fact that entry to the Church is partly achieved through baptism. In the absence of roodscreens, chancel rails or balustrades serve to separate chancels from naves. Unusually small churches, like the one at Cornwall, sometimes lack chancels and have shallow, balustraded platforms instead.

In either case, this area of the church contains the clergy stalls or chairs, the choir stalls if the church is particularly large, and the altar. Altars are placed at the eastern ends of chancels, and many are raised by three short steps symbolic of the Trinity. Most altars are backed either by dossals or reredoses. Pulpits and lecterns stand at the front of chancels. Small churches often lack pulpits and their lecterns are used for both lessons and sermons.

Although they all follow this basic arrangement, Anglican mission churches display significant regional variation in style between those built in the north and those built in the south. Two principal conditions assured that the churches of the north would be larger and generally superior to those of the southern Interior. First, the requirements and resources of the two areas differed significantly. The Indians of the north comprised larger bands, they had greater need of sizable churches, and, through income earned in the salmon industry, they had considerable wealth to bestow on their churches. In contrast, the bands of the lower Thompson and Nicola valleys were small and poor, and they had neither the funds nor the cause to build large and elaborate churches. Second, the Indians of the north had a long tradition of working in wood. The Haida, Tsimshian, and Kwakiutl people were skilled carpenters and carvers, builders of plank houses and sculptors of totems. Missionaries simply redirected their skills and enthusiasm toward building and decorating churches. The Salish of the southern Interior lacked a comparable woodworking tradition and consequently built simpler, less elegant churches.

It was not only the Anglican missionaries in British Columbia who built in the Gothic manner. Although the Gothic Revival began in Britain and was especially popular among Anglicans, interest in the style had spread throughout much of the Europeanized world by the 1860s. But where Gothic became the only truly Christian style of architecture for Anglicans, other denominations considered it simply one of several valid ecclesiastical styles. Most of British Columbia's early Roman Catholic missionaries — the neomediaevalist Oblate Fathers — were from France, where the impact of the Gothic Revival was slightly modified. They, too, built most of their churches in the Gothic style, but many of their buildings also contain fea-

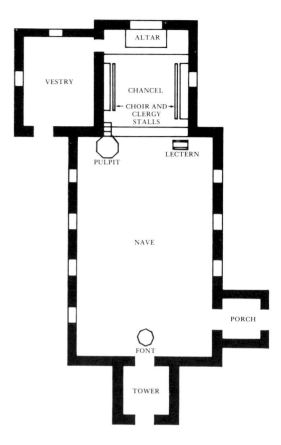

Floorplan of a well-furnished Anglican mission church

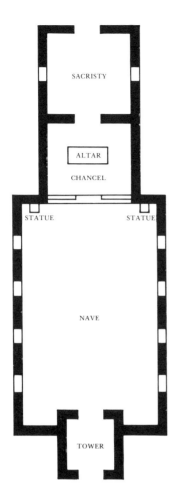

Floorplan of a typical Roman Catholic mission church

tures such as round-headed windows, pilasters, sunbursts, and dentil courses, which are drawn from the quite different Romanesque and Baroque styles. Churches built for the diocesan priests of Vancouver Island — most of whom came from Quebec — contain more of the highly Baroque features typical of Quebec churches.

Like Anglican mission churches, Oblate buildings in three areas of the province — the Okanagan and Similkameen valleys, the Kootenays and the Boundary Country, and the Fraser and Lillooet valleys — have regionally distinct features. Such regional styles evolved where local superiors established models for imitation, where individual missionaries built many churches within a single district, or where the woodworking skills of Indians were unusually advanced. Certain early churches offered guidelines for subsequent construction by natives or Oblate builders. The facades of early Oblate churches in New Westminster, for example, were imitated in mission churches throughout the lower coast and the Fraser and Lillooet valleys. Okanagan-Similkameen churches were modeled on the central church at Okanagan Mission, while church designs in the Kootenays and Boundary Country were apparently based on those of churches built at St. Eugene and Fort Steele.

The majority of these Roman Catholic mission churches followed a single floor plan which had its origins in the Middle Ages. This plan included a western tower, a nave, a sanctuary, and a sacristy. Only a few rural Roman Catholic churches in British Columbia have apses, transepts, or multiple towers. Like some Anglican and nonconformist churches, a number of Roman Catholic buildings have a belfry instead of a tower. But unlike Anglican churches, Roman Catholic buildings never have southwest porches, and sacristies are usually located behind sanctuaries rather than beside them.

The interior arrangements of Catholic mission churches are all similar. Rows of pews with kneelers fill either side of the nave. Galleries at the rear of the nave sometimes provide additional seating for choirs or large congregations. Altars and reredoses stand on the highest steps of raised sanctuaries or sanctuary platforms. Although some of the paneled or balustraded altar rails have been removed in compliance with the liturgical innovations of the Second Vatican Council, they still stand in front of most altars. A few churches have lateral altars or shrines flanking their sanctuaries. Framed prints showing the Stations of the Cross hang in the naves of most mission churches. Pulpits and lecterns are rare, since Roman Catholic worship focuses on the Celebration of the Eucharist rather than on the preaching of a sermon. Confessionals are also unusual in mission churches.

In contrast to both the Roman Catholics and the Anglicans, nonconformist missionaries — mainly from eastern Canada and Britain — were traditionally suspicious of the ritual that they associated with extreme Gothic architecture. Ontarian Methodists, for example, initially distrusted the Oxford and Cambridge Movements and, in 1860, labelled Tractarianism *the most deadly enemy to vital godliness in the Established Church of England.* Subsequent judgments were less vitriolic, but not by much. In 1884 the *Canadian Methodist Magazine* suggested that *the thousand mission services among the poor in lowly chapels and 'tabernacles' and 'conventicles', are the truer hope for ... moral regeneration ... than stately pageants in cathedral fanes.* Presbyterian and Salvation Army opinions on architecture were slightly more liberal, but they too feared the mystery and ritual associated with the Gothic manner.

As a rule, all of these nonconformist missionaries who came to British Columbia intended their churches to be functional meeting houses and places of prayer, not beautiful temples laden with symbolism. They were to be of manageable size, with uninterrupted views and good acoustics. But neither these intentions nor their general puritan traditions prevented the nonconformist missionaries on the north coast and in the valleys of the Skeena and the Nass from building churches with recognizable Gothic features. And the Methodist churches at Meanskinisht and Port Simpson were unabashedly Gothic.

The extravagance of these nonconformist exteriors probably stemmed from a combination of the Indians' interest in pageantry and the advanced woodworking skills of the north coast natives. Missionaries realized that the Indians had an inherent love of display, which was traditionally expressed in dress, the potlatch, and woodcarving. And, since Methodist, Presbyterian, and Salvation Army missionaries forbade ritual within their churches, they contented their Indian followers with display on the exterior.

Nonconformist churches have extremely simple floor plans. Most consist of a combined nave and sanctuary, with an entry porch or tower. Since the sacred functions take place at one end of the nave of nonconformist churches, none of these buildings has a chancel. The interiors of many nonconformist churches have perished unphotographed. Those that survive are generally plain and unadorned, although there are two exceptions: Kispiox has a finely decorated font and Kitseguecla an interesting series of floral paintings.

CONSTRUCTION TECHNOLOGY

British Columbia's early church architecture responded to forces both modern and traditional. The architectural styles and floor plans used by the various denominations were drawn from eastern Canadian and European traditions. But the techniques by which the missionaries built and furnished their churches in British Columbia were more usually those of industrialized North America. On a late-nineteenth-century frontier, where stone, brick, and iron were much too expensive and generally unavailable, church-builders turned to construction with wood. Although churches were often built of logs, the vast majority were balloon-frame structures.

Of all the technological innovations that influenced everyday North American construction in the nineteenth century, the balloon-frame was undoubtedly the most important. The speed and extent of its acceptance were phenomenal. Initially developed in the American Mid-West in the early 1830s, balloon-frame construction spread rapidly throughout the continent, supplanting older techniques and eventually reaching Europe and the Antipodes. Without the balloon-frame, Chicago, Denver, San Francisco, Vancouver, and thousands of western boom-towns would have been built very slowly indeed.

Simply put, balloon-frames consist of slender lightweight wooden members which are nailed together to form a rigid structure. Boards are sub-

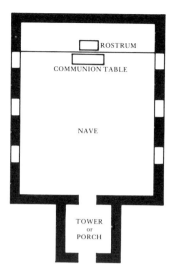

Of all the churches built in early British Columbia, Nonconformist examples were the simplest

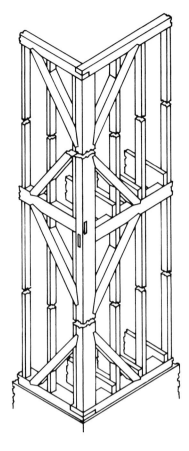

The balloon frame revolutionized building practices on the North American frontier and was readily accepted by British Columbian church builders

sequently nailed to the frame to cover it. This method is completely different from traditional construction with wood in which heavy timbers are attached to each other by mortise-and-tenon joints. Because of their simplicity and lightness, balloon-frames can be raised quickly and easily. To build a traditional, heavy-timber building of equal size, one required the labour of twenty men, some of them highly skilled. But in 1865 G. E. Woodward maintained that one man and a boy could build a balloon-frame structure without additional assistance. Savings in labour were reflected in lower costs, and expenses were reduced further as the price of materials declined. Balloon-frame construction required great volumes of precisely milled boards, and modern advances in sawmill technology permitted mass-production of these, which led to lower prices. Machine-made steel nails replaced hand-wrought ones, and their price plummeted from twenty-five cents per pound early in the nineteenth century to three cents per pound by 1842.

Cost and efficiency were the balloon-frame's inherent advantages. But certain environmental and technological conditions on the British Columbia frontier made it a particularly popular construction method with missionaries and Indians alike. First, wherever they might be, the province's missionaries had ready access to wood. Forests were always nearby, and virtually all Indian bands had wood lots of their own. Technological factors were perhaps just as important, for although many Indian villages were somewhat isolated at the time of the first missionary contact in the 1860s, and although British Columbia was a distant component of a far-flung empire, most Indians were rapidly exposed to industrial innovation. White miners, farmers, missionaries, and other settlers introduced them to new materials, tools, and building methods. In the early days, steamboats and clippers carried tools and materials and other goods from San Francisco, New York, and London, and mule trains distributed them throughout the province. With the advent of transcontinental railways and telegraphs in the 1880s links were forged with North America's industrial heartland. If British Columbia builders found materials, tools, sawmill parts, or other goods locally unavailable after that date, they only had to place orders with merchants. The province's own railways, inland waterways, pack trails, and roads could then carry freight from coastal ports to most centres inland.

Milled lumber became increasingly available as settlement by whites accelerated. Sawmills sprang up wherever miners, farmers, townsmen, and railway builders required construction materials. Since Europeans often settled near traditional Indian villages, native builders seldom had difficulty in obtaining supplies at little cost. By the 1890s only the most isolated villages lacked easy access to sawmills, and even they often managed to obtain materials. Some villages hauled lumber overland or over ice, while others rafted it on lakes and rivers. Villages adjacent to commercial sawmills obtained materials more easily. The Catholic Indians of Qua'aout near Chase sent timber from their reserve to the mill across the river at Squilax and received finished lumber in return. A few Indian villages had sawmills of their own and supplied materials to other bands nearby.

While lumber might be obtained locally by Indian builders, many items were too complicated for local craftsmen to make and had to be ordered from manufacturers on the lower mainland. A number of mills and sash-

and-door factories in these trading and manufacturing centres actively pursued ecclesiastical customers by advertising in denominational periodicals. Principal among these firms were B.C. Mills Timber and Trading and Brunette Sawmills — both of New Westminster — and Robertson and Hackett of Vancouver. All three companies were operating in the 1890s and early 1900s, the very years in which the construction of mission churches peaked. In 1896, when the Oblate priest, Father Blanchet, completed the church at Sugar Cane, he obtained his materials from the coast. As his superior, Father Le Jacq reported, *shingles, nails, doors, windows, paint, etc., etc. . . . It is necessary to order all these things from the coast, that is, from New Westminster or Vancouver, and a cost of 4 sous per pound for shipping must be added to the purchase price.*

With tools, precisely milled lumber, and other mass-produced materials so widely available for balloon-frame construction, it is perhaps remarkable that preindustrial crafts survived at all. But log churches continued to be built, though mainly in unusually isolated or poverty-stricken villages. Most were built slightly before the full onslaught of white civilization, which occurred in the 1860s and 1870s in areas near the coast and in the 1880s and 1890s in areas further inland. After 1900, few were built anywhere except in the Cariboo-Chilcotin district. The earliest ones were sometimes little more than hovels. One missionary called them *nothing else but lodges of a special form,* and described one Déné chapel as *a wretched building. . . . They built it five years ago, after the first visit of the priest while they were still very much novices at this type of construction. Between the tree trunks that form the walls are spaces large enough to admit one's hand, and, at night, one can easily see the stars through the holes in the roof.*

Most of the earliest log churches have long since disappeared, though a few of the best, including the first churches at Inkaneep and Penticton, survive in a slightly altered form. The log churches of the late nineteenth and early twentieth centuries have fared somewhat better. These were far more sophisticated, because their builders had benefited from increased exposure to white, industrial technology. If the Roman Catholic churches that remain at Cayuse Creek, Inkaneep, Penticton, Necoslie, Spahomin, and Quesnel, and the Anglican ones at Shackan and Cornwall are representative, then most log churches were dovetailed rather than saddle-notched and built of squared rather than naturally round logs. Both notching techniques were common throughout the North American frontier and were easily learned by settlers, Indians, and missionaries alike.

Log churches were necessarily small and dark. Further, their wooden nature was obvious. Though churches with squared, dovetailed logs often appeal to modern eyes, missionaries apparently preferred to disguise them. Once milled lumber became available in an area, its log churches were often covered with shiplap siding.

Balloon-frame buildings might be larger, brighter, and more elegant than churches of log, but they too had their disadvantages. Relative to those of stone churches, building dimensions were limited; and if structural stability were to be preserved, stylistic concessions had to be made. Arcades and side-aisles, for instance, had to be avoided; and the regular spacing of the balloon-frame's vertical timbers required that windows be kept small. Tech-

Dovetail corner joint

nological considerations even narrowed the choice of ceiling vaults and made it difficult to erect elaborate hammer-beam roofs. Builders sometimes failed to recognize such limitations, and iron tie-bars had to be introduced when buildings threatened to collapse.

Although about 90 percent of the province's early Indian churches were balloon-frame structures, and although many of them were attractive, many missionaries thought of them as simply expedients. They would have preferred churches of stone that more closely resembled those they had known in Europe and eastern Canada. Anglicans, especially, considered wood a *defective and inferior* material, suitable only for churches in the colonies. Roman Catholics and nonconformists seldom voiced equivalent sentiments, though this is not to say that they entirely approved of wooden buildings. Oblate builders were perhaps more realistic than the Anglicans, for wherever they worked they adapted their architecture to local conditions; and the Methodist and Presbyterian missionaries from Ontario were perfectly familiar with wooden buildings in the first place.

Although missionaries might object to wooden churches, their native congregations were generally happy with what they had. For most Indians the construction of even the smallest wooden church was a matter of great importance. As one observer wrote in 1896, *A great many little wooden churches, sometimes as far as fifty miles distant from any other town, spring up in the missions. The Indians support their own churches now, and take great delight in building them. They have been known to take such an active interest in the erection of a chapel that the hammers were heard pounding the whole night through, while the dedication of a bell in the little steeple and its first deep-toned tollings as it rung out in the keen, still atmosphere inspired the natives with a mad revelry peculiar to the race and never to be forgotten.*

Missionary participation in church building was often great. Because they wanted the churches to conform to prescribed liturgical and architectural traditions, they either gave Indian builders very specific instructions, personally supervised the initial and final stages of construction, or took up tools themselves and worked alongside native carpenters. Oblate priests and lay brethren, in particular, were often remarkably gifted craftsmen who had developed their skills by working with paid white carpenters. Two of the province's most prolific church builders — Father Le Jeune of Kamloops and Father Coccola of St. Eugene — learned balloon-frame technology from the builders of the Indian Residential School at Kamloops.

Native Indians, of course, were often master builders in their own right. Although some interior Indians had no tradition of working with wood and had to be taught by missionaries, most of the province's natives had at least some familiarity with carpentry, and the Indians of the coast were particularly skilled. Missionaries at once recognized their abilities and had little difficulty in directing native builders toward the construction of frame churches. As the Anglican clergyman the Reverend B. Appleyard noted in 1899, *The Indian is a born carpenter; as a child he takes to tools as a duck takes to water; whatever we see around us bears witness to his skill . . . [his] faculty for imitating and picking up practical knowledge is wonderful; anything [he sees] done [he] will reproduce without trouble.*

With such skilled carpenters at hand, missionaries were often content to give hand-drawn sets of building plans to native workmen who could follow them with little difficulty. As Father Le Jacq, superior of the Oblates at Fort St. James reported in 1880, *There are sixteen villages in the district, each assigned to one of six reunion centres.... We intend to built a decent chapel in each reunion centre, each large enough to contain the population. They will be modeled on the church that we have just built at [Necoslie]. On returning to their respective villages after the Christmas reunion, the various chiefs carried a little plan drawn by the Reverend Father Blanchet. We propose to square big pieces of wood and to put them together before the end of winter.* A few years later Bishop Paul Durieu described one of these churches which had been built at Stoney Creek: *The Indians aren't very inventive but they do have a genius for imitation. Before our eyes we have a perfect, small-scale reproduction of the large church of Our Lady of Good Hope at* [Necoslie].

It was not at all unusual for Indian builders to copy particular churches they had seen. When the Roman Catholic Indians of Bonaparte built a church in 1890, they based their design on the Belgian architect Joseph Bouillon's Sechelt church of 1889. Similarly, the second Anglican church at Gitlakdamix was modeled on Prince Rupert's Anglican Cathedral, built in 1912-25 to the specifications of Toronto architects Gordon and Helliwell.

As a rule, when the missionaries produced original plans for Indians to follow, they simply put their impressions of European and eastern Canadian buildings on paper. As they did so, they discarded unessential features and made minor alterations. Pattern books, parish histories, and other publications offered a wealth of architectural detail for imitation, but missionaries apparently used them not as basic plans but as sources of inspiration for decorative detail. With access to these pattern books and builders' guides, Indian craftsmen in British Columbia first armed themselves with modern chisels, fretsaws, planes, and other tools and then produced a wide variety of innovative "gingerbread" decoration for their churches.

Mission churches were furnished in an extremely piecemeal fashion. Missionary societies overseas sent money rather than goods, but even so, church funds were often completely consumed by stipends and living costs, leaving nothing for furnishing the buildings. In some instances items were donated, usually by sympathetic white settlers. But missionaries and Indians occasionally found funds from other sources with which to purchase their requirements. Among the Roman Catholics, at least, fines levied against offenders of village law went toward furnishing and beautifying the church. Paradoxically, an unusually fine church might be the result of transgression rather than piety. Whatever their sources of funds, however, Indian congregations generally purchased only those items which they could not manufacture themselves.

Since native woodworking skills varied from one village to the next, some Indians could produce furnishings that their neighbours would not even attempt to construct. There were, however, many articles that all bands had to purchase. These included factory-produced altar crosses, candlesticks, statues, altar cloths, bells, and religious pictures such as the Stations of the Cross. These items were available not only from manufacturers and distributors on the coast but also from others in Europe and in eastern North America. To avoid high freight expenses, missionaries usually purchased the largest and heaviest items from dealers within the province. Apart from building doors and window sashes, therefore, coastal manufacturers also produced confessionals, choir and chancel rails, and altars. B.C. Mills stocked *All Descriptions of Interior Finish and Church Fittings*, while Robertson and Hackett made altar-building their *specialty*.

Manufacturers from outside the province frequently advertised in mission journals and offered catalogues to potential customers. Thompson Brothers of Dublin advertised in Oblate publications and offered pulpits, altars, fonts, and mural tablets. From their factories in Montreal, Crevier and Sons, D. and J. Sadlier & Co., and R. Beullac sold a wide range of furnishings for Roman Catholic churches. English craft workshops such as Morris & Sons; Cox, Sons, and Buckley; A. R. Mowbray & Co.; and Jones and Willis & Co., provided furnishings to Anglicans the world over. British Columbia's Methodists, Presbyterians, and the Salvation Army required only a few simple furnishings. Those few that they could not obtain locally they purchased mainly from suppliers in Ontario.

The practice of buying from catalogues tended to standardize interiors. Mural tablets or pictures depicting the Last Supper, for example, embellish Roman Catholic altars at Cranbrook, D'Arcy, Shelley, Kamloops, and Enderby. Many are identical, not only to each other, but to tablets elsewhere in the country as well.

Some furnishings and fittings were standardized across denominational lines. Bells, especially, were no respecters of sect. A few came from France or England, but most were cast by foundaries in Cincinnati, Baltimore, and Troy, New York. Oblate priests openly endorsed Blymyer Bells of Cincinnati and described the company as suppliers *to all our missions up the country*. When Anglicans and nonconformists required bells, they too patronized the same companies, for the foundries advertised in both Roman Catholic and Protestant publications.

Sash-and-door factories in the lower mainland and Victoria not only supplied completed items but also contributed to church furnishings manufactured in the villages. For particularly skilled craftsmen, the fabrication of pews, altars, and balustrades was relatively easy, and most villages had access to the skilled labour of paid white carpenters, Indian wood carvers, or gifted missionaries. But native craftsmen could not always make every component they wanted to use in their own work. The factories then supplied standardized *Posts, Balusters, and all kinds of Turned Work . . . , Spiral and Fluted Turned Work, Machine-turned Head and Corner Blocks, Rosette and Base Blocks*. Carpenters could choose whichever components appealed to them and then assemble them into altars, reredoses, balustrades, and other items that they had designed themselves. In some instances, Indian craftsmen were so successful that their products were virtually indistinguishable from those professionally manufactured.

It was this combination of native craftsmanship with industrialized production that gave British Columbia's early Indian churches much of their character. Missionaries preserved the essential plans, styles, and decorations of European and eastern Canadian churches. But frontier conditions required that their buildings be small and less complex. Wood had to take the place of masonry and iron. As skilled Indians builders gained access to the tools, techniques, and materials of the industrial revolution, however, they created churches that were far from being simply replicas in wood of buildings in their missionaries' homelands.

The Villages and the Churches Today

JOHN VEILLETTE, GARY WHITE

Beaded altar frontal, Hazelton

Today, as in precontact times, many of the Indian people of British Columbia live in small scattered settlements. Although these villages are separated from the rest of the province by legal and other boundaries, they are in many ways little different from most other communities. Despite subtle differences, Indians have the same hopes and needs and the same social problems as other citizens. In many villages traces or even considerable portions of the old Indian culture remain. Native artists, in particular, keep alive the traditions of carving, weaving, and beading. At the same time, many of the churches from the early contact period still stand, and they continue to be important for many villagers, especially in the north of the province. Despite the support of their congregations, however, few of these buildings now occupy the same position in the minds of the villagers that they did when they were built.

The Indian villages lie on reserves that were gradually established around existing centres of population as white settlement spread throughout the province. By the time of the 1916 Royal Commission on Indian Affairs the pattern was nearly complete, with 231 bands living on 1900 reserves. The number of reserves seems large, but many of them were very small indeed and were only created to safeguard such traditionally important sites as burial and fishing grounds. Whereas, in earlier times elsewhere in North America, the normal practice when establishing reserves was to move separate groups of native people into new larger settlements, the system followed in British Columbia artificially perpetuated the precontact settlement pattern. Even as the reserves were being set up, the way of life on which that pattern had been based was in the process of becoming impractical. The bands could no longer move freely through the province to hunt and fish, and successively larger numbers of white settlers were using the land, the rivers, and the wildlife they supported for their own benefit. Since 1916 some of the smallest and most isolated Indian groups have amalgamated with larger ones. As a result, there were 191 bands in 1963. But despite these amalgamations, the villages still tend to be too small to form self-sufficient communities. Of the 191 bands, only 15 had more than 600 members, only 42 had more than 300, and 68 had less than 100 members.

Although most villages are now served by postal rural routes, many communities have no post office, no gas station, no bank, and no restaurant. General stores exist in only a few of the larger settlements, but some villagers operate convenience stores out of their homes. Their stock is similar to that of city neighbourhood corner groceries, but supplies of such perishables as meat, dairy products, and produce are often severely restricted or non-existent. Their shelf-life is simply too short for the volume of business in-

24

volved. Sometimes a corner in one of these stores is given over to a pool table or pinball machine to provide evening entertainment for the young men of the village. Since the stores are also popular during the daytime, the men and women who run them are usually well informed about village news.

Banking and most shopping is normally carried out in a nearby white community, where the Indian villagers will also go for automobile repairs and gasoline. Many of the people living on reserves own cars which in a high proportion of villages have come to be regarded as necessities. Horsedrawn vehicles are still to be seen, however, especially in the Cariboo and Chilcotin.

Even the smaller villages often have a community or "band" hall. These are mainly meeting and recreation buildings, but during the day they are frequently used for nursery-school programmes or regular clinics run by public health nurses. During the evening, when they are not booked for village meetings or elections, they are used for bingo, dances, child and adult recreation programmes, and community-group fund-raising events such as potluck suppers. The community hall often houses the band office, the administrative centre for all villages of any size. A band manager hired by the elected chief councillor and councillors works out of the band office and handles all employment, housing, recreation, and social-welfare programmes in the village. The elected officials have responsibilities very similar to those of a mayor, alderman, and clerk of the council. Their number varies according to the band's population.

Although nearly all the villages share these very general characteristics, day-to-day lifestyles in particular settlements vary according to the villages' location and size and whether employment is available. Some Indian villages such as North Vancouver, Musqueam, and Penticton are very near or surrounded by larger, urban communities. In this situation the traditional hunting, fishing, and gathering way of life can no longer survive, and its place is taken by the lifestyle of the surrounding community. Most houses in these villages have a television antenna, and cars are parked in most driveways. However, because the villages are separate entities and because they usually lack commercial development, they often form peaceful rural islands in hectic urban settings. Property-line fences are not common in these or any other Indian communities, and the landscape is less oppressively manicured than in the city. These features, combined with variety in lot size and fairly unsystematic placement of the houses on their lots, add to the rural atmosphere of otherwise semiurban settlements.

Other villages such as Canoe Creek and Redstone are very much more isolated. In the extreme cases of Kincolith and Fort Babine, access is possible only by boat and plane. Rough dirt and gravel roads are the usual links between these communities and the main highway, and many of the Indian settlements are not marked on the road maps or even listed in the gazetteer published by the federal government. In these villages the pace of life is slower, and the traditional cultural patterns are stronger. Here the hunting-and-fishing lifestyle often persists to some extent and provides an important source of food; but almost everywhere home-grown potatoes have replaced the customary gathered edible roots in the native diet. Sometimes logging and ranching supplement the older way of life, and, on the coast, the traditional fishing economy has been expanded; many of the men now own and

Haying at Glen Vowell

Typical village housing at isolated Fort Babine

25

operate commercial fishing boats. But few of these isolated villages are prosperous, and, unfortunately, many of the more aggressive men and women have left for larger centres of population, where schools and other services are more readily available.

Summer occupations in most villages are dominated by berry-picking and the fish runs. Berries, like fish, are canned or frozen and then stored. Much of the fish is also smoked to preserve it. The fishermen cut the fish into thin strips and hang the strips in the smokehouses. These buildings, which look like windowless sheds, are familiar sights in the coastal fishing villages.

If a village is located in an area where employment is available, many of the men have steady jobs. In villages like Kitwanga with two lumber mills and several logging companies nearby, some of the villagers have been able to build fine homes. Sometimes in such communities the women work in restaurants, stores, and hotels. They also find seasonal employment such as tree planting and fish processing when a forestry operation or cannery is close by.

Television has invaded most of the homes in many villages, and it often provides the main evening entertainment. Radio is taken for granted. Movies are sometimes shown in the community hall or they are seen during the weekend shopping trip to the nearest town. There, on Friday and Saturday nights, while the younger people enjoy the movies, play pool, or talk, the beer parlour becomes for some the social hub of the village. Among other forms of entertainment, sports are very popular, and many villages hold regular sports days which have developed into intervillage competitions. In many areas of the province villagers participate in regional Indian basketball and soccer tournaments, and during the summer many of the Cariboo and Chilcotin people hold their own rodeos and take part in events like the Williams Lake Stampede. Rodeo grounds, baseball diamonds, or soccer fields are part of nearly every village landscape.

One of the most noticeable features of native communities is the standardized housing advocated and subsidized by the federal government. Houses in Indian villages across the province have a similar appearance, although, in areas where employment is available, houses have more variety and individuality. In nearly all villages, if and when the houses are painted, the villagers prefer to use bright lively colours. Older houses remain in some villages, and, on the north coast, especially, a number of fine examples exist, complete with decorative woodwork in the late Victorian manner. In the Interior, these older houses are usually less imposing and typically, throughout the province, the church is the only building in the village with strong vertical emphasis and individuality in what looks like an unlandscaped modern subdivision of low, plain houses without paved streets.

The exteriors of the churches are more often maintained than the interiors. Occasionally, the complete building may be raised and set on new concrete foundations, but apart from this, changes are usually superficial and simply involve replacing the original shingles with asphalt or aluminum roofing. The original exterior doors and front steps have also often been replaced. Modern slab doors are the usual replacements, and they mar the composition of the building's facade. The upper tower and spire of the churches are often left unpainted while the rest of the building receives two or three suc-

Ornate older house in Gitlakdamix

cessive repaintings. Christmas lights frequently remain strung on the facade for many seasons.

The interiors of the churches are often changed. Even where there are no structural alterations inside the building, the decorations often include modern plastic flowers, Christmas trimmings, and plastic curtains. The most common renovations involve covering the original floor with tiles, sheet linoleum, or carpet, sheathing the original walls with plywood paneling, and covering the ceiling with pressed paper tiles. In buildings where the original ceiling was high, a lower false ceiling is sometimes added to make the interior lighter and easier to heat. Modern oil furnaces or electric heaters frequently replace the old wood stoves.

In villages such as Alkali Lake, Shulus, Stony Creek, and Fort Babine, the church remains the physical focus of the village, but in others, like Cranbrook and Kamloops, the church now stands by itself in a widely scattered settlement. When they were built, all the churches were at the village centres, but the focus of some communities has shifted as they have grown dependent on the business of the towns for their employment and supplies.

On the north coast the villages, which are mainly Anglican, are larger than average and often have resident priests. Elsewhere in the province, many of the larger Roman Catholic villages also support a resident priest, and these churches have services once a week. Where the community is too small, a traveling priest — generally Oblate in the north and remote areas, diocesan in other regions — now holds regular services only once a month. He will also hold special services for weddings, baptisms, and funerals.

Church festivals are no longer public holidays in the way that they once were, and there are no longer great religious gatherings as at the passion plays held in Mission when the early churches were being built. Some church events are still well attended, however, and when a new bell tower at Kitwanga was blessed in 1974 people came to join in with the festivities from all the surrounding villages. In the north coast villages, especially, there are numerous revival-like services held in the community halls every winter. These are interdenominational and consist mainly of hymn-singing and testimonials. Occasionally parishes hold retreats and other special services to strengthen the faith and reaffirm the commitment of their congregations.

Many congregations throughout the province organize harvest sales, bazaars, and suppers which are attended by the majority of their communities. In this way they raise funds from irregular churchgoers to maintain the church buildings. Sunday schools are often active, too, and a number of church camps provide diversion for the children during the summer holidays.

While the fortunes of the native people seem to be rising, not many Indian congregations support their churches as strongly as they did in the early days. However, church attendance in the early days was sometimes encouraged if not enforced by village law and backed up by fines. Those who attend church now do so because they wish to, and there is often a noticeable sincerity and strength in the services in native churches. Perhaps as they put the last century into historical perspective and decide what they chose to accept and what was forced upon them, the Indian people of British Columbia may decide that their churches are, after all, an important — though adopted — aspect of their culture.

Modernized church interior at Nazko

Indian passion play at Mission, c. 1890

Southern Coast and Fraser Valley

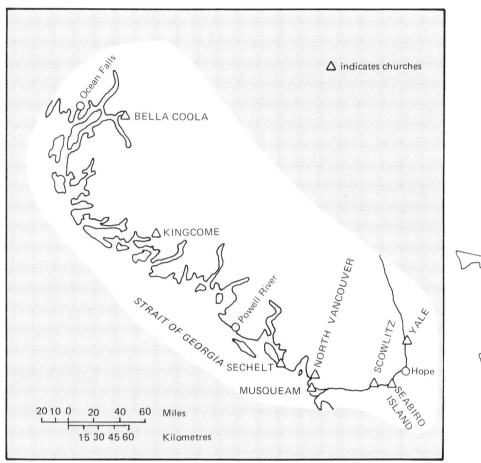

North of Hope the Fraser River flows through a steep-sided valley in the coastal mountain range. On nearing the Strait of Georgia the river deposits sediments to form a broad, fertile delta. North of the delta, numerous fjords or inlets pierce the mountainous coastline.

Temperatures in the region are mild throughout the year, varying between freezing point in winter and a summer mean of about 16° C (60° F). Summer maximums in the southwestern part of the region are frequently higher. Inland, up the Fraser Valley, the temperature range is somewhat greater, and winters are cooler in the northern part of the region, near Bella Coola. Annual precipitation is moderate, averaging 85 – 112 cm. (35 – 45″) on the coast, and declines slightly towards the Interior. At some locations on the coast, however, annual precipitation reaches 250 cm. (100″). Ninety per cent falls as rain.

Forests of hemlock, cedar, and Douglas fir cover the mountainsides both on the coast and inland. Deciduous trees such as alder and poplar line the river valleys. Edible roots and berries are abundant. Game is plentiful, and an extremely large run of salmon travels up the Fraser each year.

In many respects, Coast Salish material culture and social structure resembled those of the coastal groups to the north. Like the Bella Coola, the Kwakiutl, and the Tsimshian, the Coast Salish lived in semipermanent, plank-house villages and practised a form of potlatch. But Coast Salish group organization, winter ceremonies, and art were decidedly less elaborate. Traditionally, Coast Salish economic activities centred on the salmon run, their major source of food, and, today, many still rely on the sea and river for part of their food and income.

Under the direction of Roman Catholic missionaries, some of the most ornate and impressive churches in the province were built in this area at Sechelt, Musqueam, and North Vancouver. The buildings at Musqueam and Sechelt shared many features with a larger group of Roman Catholic churches that extended into the Lillooet-Brigade Trail region. Their major distinguishing features were very tall, many-sided spires.

Emmanuel Church

UNITED (FORMERLY METHODIST)
BELLA COOLA

Built c. 1905

Before 1850 the Bella Coola, the Kim-
squint, and Talio tribes inhabited
several villages in the area of what is
now called the Bella Coola Valley. But

the smallpox epidemic of the mid-nineteenth century decimated the Indian population of the region, and when the missionaries arrived in the area in the early 1880s the only major village left was Bella Coola. Edward Nichols and his wife, the first resident missionaries, arrived in Bella Coola in 1886. Before they moved away in 1895 they saw a little church built (p. 31). It was characterized by an extremely uncomplicated bell tower and angular pointed windows set only in the facade. By 1900 the simple building no longer satisfied either the congregation or the minister, Thomas Neville, who had succeeded Mr. Nichols. By 1906 they had built and dedicated the new Emmanuel Church. Since then, like many rural Indian churches, it has undergone considerable upheaval.

During the 1920s, after several severe floods, the villagers moved across the river from the original site of the village. In the 1930s they moved the church as well. They began by removing the church tower, after which they used two caterpillars to drag the remainder of the building through the forest to the river. Once there, they floated the church across the water on a raft and placed it on a new foundation at its present site (bottom). Its tower was rebuilt according to the original plan.

It is a fairly large church, and the bellcast roof of the tower is attractively designed but the pointed windows are all curiously wide and low and lack vertical thrust. The main front window is a good example of this weakness. Similarly, the severe and uninteresting louvred openings of the tower could have been located far more gracefully than they were.

St. George's Church

ANGLICAN

KINGCOME

Built 1930

It must have been a grand occasion when Bishop de Pencier in 1939 dedicated both a church and a totem pole at Kingcome. The totem pole was erected in honour of King George VI, and the church named for England's patron saint.

Kingcome is well known as the setting for Margaret Craven's book *I Heard the Owl Call My Name*. In the 1930s the village had a population of around four hundred, but today it is much smaller.

St. George's Church (1955 photo) is on the banks of the Quee River and stands against the background of Whoop-su, or Noisy Mountain. On the whole, the building was constructed in the classic English style found at St. Peter's, Hazelton (p. 76). But not all of its features were in complete accord with the dominant style; triple-arched louvred openings in the tower, the tower decoration, the arched windows, and the entrance design are all departures. Rot caused by the wet coastal climate made it necessary to rebuild the tower in 1959.

The building to the rear of the church is the rectory.

Our Lady of the Rosary Church

ROMAN CATHOLIC

SECHELT

Built 1889-90

In 1860 the Indians living at Sechelt drove away two Roman Catholic priests. But two years later they changed their attitude and requested a missionary. After nine more years the band was completely converted, and by the late 1880s Sechelt had become the Roman Catholic missionaries' model settlement in British Columbia.

Three churches were erected in Sechelt within this brief period. The first, built in 1868, was probably a simple log structure. A second and larger building named the Church of the Most Holy Redeemer replaced it in 1872 because the congregation had outgrown the first. Work on the third church, Our Lady of the Rosary (top), began in 1889, and in June 1890, when the building was blessed and dedicated by the bishop of New Westminster, Bishop Paul Durieu, the community became a showplace for Indians and missionaries alike.

Indians from interior bands traveled by train and boat at specially reduced fares to participate in the dedication ceremony. They returned to their villages with news of Sechelt's achievements and first-hand accounts of the new church's magnificence. In one case at least, the building at Sechelt was used as direct inspiration: the complicated spire at Bonaparte (p. 134) is clearly a copy of the spires here, and a version of the arched gable treatment was used on the back gable at Bonaparte.

Joseph Bouillon, a Belgian-born Vancouver architect, designed Our Lady of the Rosary to seat a congregation of four hundred. With a full range of materials at his disposal, a generous, even lavish, budget, and professional craftsmen available to supervise construction, he was able to build a church

quite unlike most of those found in Indian villages. The Vancouver *Daily World* reported that *all the work for the new church was done by the Indians themselves under the direction of ... the architect* (4 June 1890), but other skilled craftsmen were called in and much of the woodwork was not locally made. A Mr. Alfred Cook and a Mr. H. Gain, both of Vancouver, are on record as painter and plasterer, respectively; and Vancouver millwork shops almost certainly provided not only the windows, doors, and furnishings, but also the factory-produced materials used in the airy colonnade supporting the arch of the facade gable and in the bracketed dentil cornice of the lower eaves. Under professional direction, and with machine-made supplies, the Sechelt villagers probably provided only the general labour needed.

Describing the church from the outside as *of a very handsome design having a gay and cheerful appearance, with elaborate and tasteful decorations*, the *Daily World* reporter then turned his attention to the interior (top), calling it *still more beautifully and elaborately finished than the exterior.* Certainly, it was as finished as any urban parish church, and to this end Bouillon adapted many of his exterior decorative motifs for use in the interior: in the sanctuary, for example, both the altar rail and the altar front achieved light arcade effects like those of the facade. Bouillon was also prepared to transpose and adapt features from urban housebuilding into the ecclesiastical context. Just as the arched gable treatment of the facade was a common feature of contemporary urban domestic architecture, so the kind of fret bracket supporting the statues of angels on each side of the altar was more commonly found decorating the veranda-posts of late-nineteenth-century private houses.

In January 1906 Our Lady of the
Rosary burned, and, after a year,
another church (top and bottom), took
its place. Dedicated to Our Lady of
Lourdes, it had an unusual false-front
facade and a tower over 125 feet high
which could be seen from Nanaimo.
Professionals undoubtedly played as
large a role in constructing it as they
had in building its predecessor. In
October 1970 this church, too, was
destroyed by fire.

A passage describing Sechelt in 1895
gives an idea of the impression the
village made before the turn of the century while Our Lady of the Rosary still
stood. *After a four hours trip* [from
Vancouver by boat] *we came in sight of
the Sechelt village. There it lies on the
beach of a broad bay. It has two rows of
white houses, about a quarter of a mile
long. In the centre stands the church, a
large edifice of romanesque style, with
its facade flanked with two elegant
towers. Tall pines and fir trees encircle
the village and form a picturesque
background. The foreground is made by
the round white line of the sandy beach,
with a narrow strip of green in front of
the first row of houses.*

St. Paul's Church
ROMAN CATHOLIC
NORTH VANCOUVER
Built 1909-10

Until recently this very well-known church was such a prominent feature on the shore of North Vancouver that it was officially designated as a landmark for ships entering the harbour.

The original building on the same site was a temporary chapel erected in 1866. It was the first Roman Catholic church built in what is now Greater Vancouver. A single-spired church took its place in 1884, and, in 1909, transepts were added to the nave, twin spires replaced the single one, and the church was thoroughly remodeled in the Gothic style. After these changes were complete, the church was rededicated and named St. Paul's after Bishop Paul Durieu, the bishop under whose direction the Roman Catholic Indian missions reached their peak of development in British Columbia. St. Paul's Hospital in Vancouver is also named after him.

Despite the popularity of the Gothic style for early rural churches in British Columbia, St. Paul's is the only Roman Catholic example showing such complete fidelity to the original models. Its cruciform plan and twin-spired facade are common to most of the original Gothic churches; the gables with parapets, the pointed and round windows,

the profusion of buttresses, and the steep, high, octagonal tower roofs with dormers are all typical of the style.

Although the predominant design influence is Gothic, the fretwork decoration in the pediments above the doors is completely original and owes nothing to any particular architectural style.

Similar fretwork once decorated the interior, especially the altar rails and the reredos of the main altar. It has now been removed, and the present altar rails are of iron, giving a much more open impression. Earlier complex paneling on the lower walls has similarly given way to simple modern plywood panels, and textured white paint now covers the plaster of the walls and vaulted ceiling. This elaborate interior finish was consistent with the grand design of the exterior, but its Gothic aspects were not so pronounced.

St. Michael the Archangel

ROMAN CATHOLIC

MUSQUEAM

Built 1902

Although it is now almost engulfed by the city of Vancouver, in 1900 Musqueam was very much in the country, and even in 1928, when C. F. Newcombe photographed the village and church (above), the rural feeling was strong.

Twin-spired churches are uncommon in British Columbia, and the particularly handsome pair at St. Michael's was outstanding. Their design was similar to that of the spire at Scowlitz (p. 42), but here it was more fully developed and enhanced by pinnacles at the base of the towers. The gables of the drum, decorated with fretwork bargeboards and hearts with seven swords, symbolic of the Seven Sorrows of Our Lady, were refinements which added to the building's appeal but did not take away from the overall strength of its design. A statue of St. Michael rested in a niche over the door, a feature reminiscent of the churches of Quebec and larger urban churches.

One of the spires of the church at Musqueam was destroyed in a storm in the late 1940s or early 1950s, and in August 1963, the building burned when a grass fire ran out of control.

Church of St. Mary

ROMAN CATHOLIC

SCOWLITZ

Built c. 1900

Facing the Fraser River near Harrison
Hot Springs, St. Mary's is a simple,
elegant building with strong vertical
lines. Similar in some ways to the spires
at both Musqueam (p. 40) and
Skookumchuck (p. 117), this spire has
wide trim centred under each of its
gables, which creates the effect of vertical arrows within the tall slim points of
the segments of spire roof. Sections of
scalloped shingles typical of the 1890-
1900 period relieve the roof's surface by
adding textural variety.

One might expect the angular pointed
windows found here to be common in a
rural environment where simplification
of urban designs tends to be the rule.
But by the time British Columbia's
interior churches were built, Vancouver and Victoria sash-and-door
factories were already making the
standard curved version easily available.
As a result the windows at Scowlitz, far
from being the norm, are distinctly
unusual.

Only two or three families now live in
Scowlitz; the church is abandoned and
moving closer to ruin with each year
that passes. In removing the cove siding
to the right of the tower, vandals have
revealed the diagonal sheathing generally used in early well-built frame structures (see p. 70). The same vandals
were probably the ones responsible for
destroying all of St. Mary's interior
fittings and furniture. The remains,
however, suggest that these furnishings
were neither particularly fine nor
elaborate.

Roman Catholic Church

SEABIRD ISLAND

n.d.

The Seabird Island settlement near Agassiz was formed after 1850 by members of the Popkum, Squawtits, Ohamil, Skawahlook, Hope, and Yale tribes. Before then, these groups had lived in many smaller villages, and their tribal boundaries were relatively unfixed.

Photographed in 1949 shortly before its destruction — it was replaced by a new building — the church had a sagging roof caused by rot in the foundation. Its arched windows were glazed with coloured glass, and the octagonal spire, although plain, was given interest by a scrolled cornice and bands of pointed shingles.

St. Joseph's Church

ROMAN CATHOLIC

YALE

Built c. 1900

St. Joseph's is set amid splendid scenery
where the Fraser Valley narrows. A very
plain structure, it was built forty years
after the boom of the 1860s, when Yale
became an outpost of the Fraser mission
(centred on St. Charles's, New
Westminster).

Yale grew enormously during the
Gold Rush because it was the highest
navigable point on the Fraser, and the
miners bound for the Cariboo goldfields
would disembark there to set out on the
Royal Engineers' road to the north. By
the time this church was built, the
settlement's importance was already
greatly reduced. Like many rural
wooden churches in the province,
St. Joseph's has few features besides
tower, spire, and bull's eye window to
suggest that it has anything to do with a
church. The tower, interestingly, looks
as though it was never designed to carry
a bell; although there is a bell, there
are no openings for the sound.

Vancouver Island

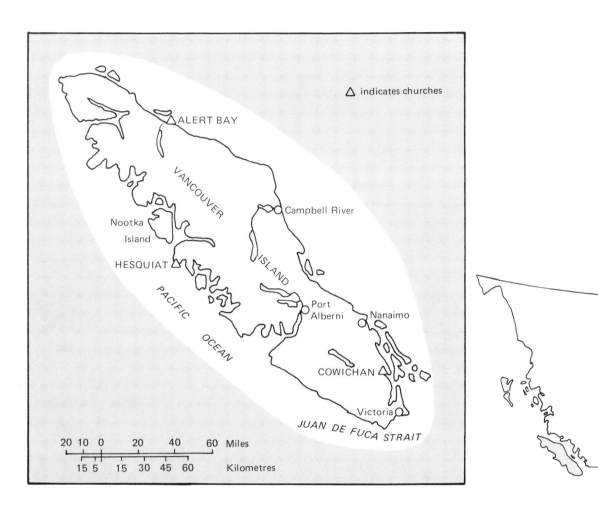

Much of Vancouver Island is rugged and mountainous, with elevations reaching 2100 metres (7000 feet). Numerous bays and fjords indent the western coastline; at the southeastern tip of the island, near Victoria, elevation descends gradually through rolling hills to the sea. Several large lakes are found in the central valleys of the island.

Temperatures on the island's western coast are mild, ranging between means of 2° C and 16° C (35° F and 60° F) over the year. Rainfall is heavy and generally exceeds 250 cm. (100″) annually. The island's eastern coast is drier and warmer — temperatures are higher by 3 – 5° C (5 – 10° F).

Red and yellow cedar predominate in the island's dense coniferous forests. Temperate rain-forest conditions occur along the west coast, where a dense undergrowth of ferns and salal makes foot passage difficult. Berries and edible fruits are plentiful, as are fish, such as salmon and cod, and sea mammals, such as seals and several species of whale.

First of the native groups to be contacted by missionaries, the Coast Salish people lived on the southeast of the island. On the west coast the Nootka

45

lived by fishing from temporary summer villages before returning in winter to isolated, self-contained villages cut off from each other by the dense forests and rocky terrain. The Kwakiutl, who lived in the northeast, had a rigidly organized social structure, similar in many respects to those of the Haida and Tsimshian. After the spring, summer, and fall food-gathering was completed, the Kwakiutl spent the winter like the north coast groups in lengthy and elaborate ceremonies and potlatches. Fishing and forestry are the major sources of income today.

Anglican missionaries converted the Kwakiutl, and the church at Alert Bay remains an impressive example of the Anglican missionary style. Unfortunately, almost none of the churches dating from early Roman Catholic contact with the Coast Salish and Nootka in the west and south of the island has survived the damp of the coastal climate.

Christic Church
ANGLICAN
ALERT BAY
Built 1892

Alert Bay is on Cormorant Island in Broughton Strait, off the mouth of the Nimpkish River. It was named in 1860 after H.M.S. *Alert*, a corvette on the Esquimalt Station from 1858 to 1861.

The Reverend A. J. Hall, the missionary in charge of Alert Bay when Christ Church was built, began his service in British Columbia at Metlakatla with Duncan. And it was at Duncan's direction that he began work on Vancouver Island. He first established a mission at Beaver Harbour, but in 1881 he moved it to Alert Bay where there was already a wharf and a store.

By 1887, Hall had established a school and a sawmill, and in 1892 he also built Christ Church. In its original state it was a remarkable building, principally because of its complex trim. Not only was the roof cresting impressively ornate, but the eaves were trimmed with equally elaborate fretwork, and quoins decorated both the corners of the building and the surrounds of the windows. Duplicating stone forms in wood to the extent of adding imitation quoins was a common feature of elaborate homebuilding in the late nineteenth century, but it was unusual in rural church buildings. The exterior of the church as a whole, with its side entrance and large, leaded, coloured glass windows in both the facade and sanctuary, had a particularly English flavour.

When Christ Church was reroofed, the eave trim was left, but the cresting and the curved vents of the original roof were removed.

The austere interior is far simpler than the exterior. Arched timbers resting on corbels repeat the arches of the windows. The pews are of a plain design, but the altar rails are unusual in having ball-turned balusters above a border of pierced crosses.

The Reverend Arthur William Corker was the clergyman in charge of Alert Bay when this photograph was taken. Between 1913 and 1925 he served as missionary to Christ Church and as principal of the Indian boy's school and Indian girl's home. Visible to his left is a banner in Kwakwalla that translates as *I Am the Redeemer*.

Sacred Heart Church

ROMAN CATHOLIC

HESQUIAT

Blessed 1893

The mission at Hesquiat on the west
coast of Vancouver Island was founded
in 1875 by Father Joseph Brabant, a
Belgian priest who had arrived in
Victoria in 1869. With the help of
Father Pierre Rondeault and Noel
LeClaire, a French-Canadian carpenter,
the first church (not shown) was ready
for service in July 1875. The lumber
used came from the cargo of the *Edwin*,
wrecked nearby on its way to Australia.

When this building, intended only for
temporary service according to Father
Brabant, became inadequate in about
1890, he collected funds for a new one
while visiting Belgium. And in 1891,
after he had returned, he noted that
*Two French Canadian carpenters
arrived here last month on the schooner*
Favorite, *loaded with building material,
in order to build our new church at
Hesquiat. On account of the general
boom in British Columbia the wages are
very high, my men being paid three
dollars and fifty cents per day (each)
and their board. The plan of the new
church was made by Stephen Donovan,
of Victoria, but was considerably modified on account of lack of means to put
up a building such as he had designed.*

Although the plan was modified, the
church as completed imitated the Gothic
style more consistently than was usual in
rural buildings. It was not common to
find either stepped buttresses or gables
with parapets on a rural wooden church
in British Columbia.

Above the nave roofline, the tower became octagonal and was finished with a dentil cornice, above which was a delicate arcaded drum. A high bellcast roof decorated with bands of scalloped shingles completed the facade. Gables identical to those used on the facade decorated the short transepts on each side near the sanctuary.

Much of the stylish and professional quality of this design was later lost when the buttresses were modified to form plain pilasters and vertical boards took the place of the herringbone pattern of the original paneled doors. Above the arched entrance, the bull's eye window was covered by a sign painted with a cross.

Wooden buildings do not survive well in the high rainfall and humidity on the west coast of Vancouver Island. In the early 1920s the spire of this church was removed because of decay, and in 1936 the whole building was razed.

St. Anne's Church

ROMAN CATHOLIC

COWICHAN

Built 1870

In 1858 Father Pierre Rondeault came
to live among the Cowichan Indians,
and by the following year he was able
with their assistance to build a log
church on Comiaken Hill. This building
served for ten years until 1869, when
Father Rondeault began construction of
a spacious stone church, sixty-four feet
long, thirty feet wide, with walls just
over sixteen feet high. The fine-grained
sandstone used to build the church was
roughly quarried by the Indians from
Comiaken Hill and carried to the site.
William Williams, a Victoria stone-
mason, performed the skilled shaping
work. The church was completed before
the end of September 1870, and it
became known as the "Butter Church"
because Father Rondeault paid his
workmen with income from the sale of
butter from his farm.

In nearly every respect, this building
imitated a parish church from Father
Rondeault's native Quebec, and it was
the only stone Indian village church in
British Columbia. Bishop Modeste
Demers consecrated the church in
November 1870, and services were held
there until 1880. At that date the congregation moved to a new and larger
church which was also dedicated to St.
Anne. When the butter church was
abandoned, its doors and windows were
taken out and transferred to various
other churches in the diocese, but the
building itself was kept in repair until
about 1930. After then, it was allowed
to fall into ruin. It has since been
partially restored.

North Coast

The westernmost part of this region includes numerous small islands, as well as the larger, mountainous Queen Charlotte Islands, where elevations reach 1200 metres (4000 feet). Hundreds of inlets cut deeply into the coast of the mainland. Two major rivers — the Skeena and the Nass — run through the coastal mountain range and drain a broad inland plateau.

A temperate but damp maritime climate prevails on the west coast of the Queen Charlotte Islands. Annual rainfall reaches 375 cm. (150″) in some locations and temperatures are mild, generally ranging between 2° C and 16° C (35° F and 60° F), although winter minimums may drop below freezing on occasion. Precipitation decreases on the leeward side of the islands, on the coast of the mainland, and inland up the valleys. Temperatures are more extreme in the river valleys and on the Interior plateau. A few areas experience below-freezing temperatures for as many as five months during the year.

Most of this mountainous terrain is covered with coastal forest. Such wild-life as bear and deer traditionally formed sources of food, together with berries and edible roots. Both the Skeena and the Nass have large salmon runs, and the Nass also has a run of oolichan (candlefish), which coastal tribes used — and still use — as a source of oil and grease and as a foodstuff. The Haida people of the Queen Charlotte Islands were dependent on the sea for much of their food supply. After contact with Europeans, they became great hunters of the sea otter for trade until the species became virtually extinct through overexploitation. Today, many Haida are involved — as are many members of the mainland tribes — in the lumber and fishing industries.

Three cultural subgroups of the larger Tsimshian language group live in different areas of the mainland: the Tsimshian along the coast, the Gitksan along the upper Skeena, and the Nishga on the Nass. All of these groups, as well as the Haida, traditionally spent the winter months in permanent vil-lages of large, cedar-planked houses, where they performed elaborate cere-monies and rituals and hosted neighbouring bands.

Anglican, Methodist, and Salvation Army missionaries shared in con-verting the people of this region. Partly because of an advanced woodwork-ing tradition among the native people, the churches built in the area were consistently handsome and elegant. Many had finely decorated Gothic towers, stained glass, delicate window tracery, and carefully crafted interiors, often of warm, naturally finished wood.

Church of St. John the Evangelist

ANGLICAN

MASSET

Dedicated 1887

The Reverend William Collison was one of the major Anglican missionary figures in northern British Columbia. He worked for three years with Duncan at Metlakatla, and before moving to Masset in 1876 he traveled once from Metlakatla to the Queen Charlotte Islands by dugout canoe with a Tsimshian crew to explore the possibilities for a mission to the Haida.

Although opposition to Collison at Masset was strong, he (and later the Reverend Charles Harrison) eventually established a school and mission, using an old, abandoned, traditional Indian plank house. This building eventually became damp and dilapidated as well as overcrowded, and by 1887 a church was completed (top).

This building was designed in a simplified version of the Anglican Gothic. It was much less elaborate than many north coast mission churches, particularly those on the Skeena and Nass. The double-arched windows were archaic; double-hung, single-arched sashes were the rule in most of the later wooden churches. The interior (bottom), however, with its scissor-truss ceiling had both the warmth and the refinement characteristic of the churches of the area.

This church was superseded by a new and much larger St. John's dedicated in February 1921 (top). The new building, with its crenellated tower and row of buttresses on each side, was more impressive on the exterior than the old one, but it lacked the charm of its predecessor. The building still exists, but the crenellated tower has been replaced, and the stained-glass window has disappeared.

St. Paul's Church

ANGLICAN

METLAKATLA

Dedicated 1874

In 1862 William Duncan led a small group of his Indian followers away from Fort Simpson to the site of the Tsimshian tribes' old village. There he founded the new Christian community of Metlakatla which eventually became one of the most celebrated of all Anglican missions.

Metlakatla became famous because Duncan created there, in a remarkably short time, a working imitation of a "civilized" European village. Houses like those in Duncan's native England stood in neat rows at right angles to the water, and a uniformed Indian police force maintained law and order.

On the one hand Duncan aimed to isolate Metlakatla from harmful European influences; on the other he tried to imitate European customs. A policy of industrial and industrious self-sufficiency was therefore natural, and Metlakatla soon boasted a fur-trading store, a sawmill, a blacksmith's shop, a soap factory, and a furniture factory.

As much as possible of the work for the church was done in Metlakatla itself. At the time it was finished, St. Paul's (top) was reputed to be the largest church west of Chicago and north of San Francisco, seating about twelve hundred people. Dramatically set on a hill above the other buildings, it dominated the village and fairly bristled with gables. The many buttresses served to support the weight of such a large roof. Along the roof ridge, extremely pronounced cresting repeated the angular lines of the gables and so intensified the building's sharp-edged appearance. Tall, narrow casement windows with rounded upper sashes were made in the village's furniture factory and mounted generously in both the sides and the facade.

As part of Duncan's plan for a self-sufficient community, he made numerous extended trips to England specifically to teach himself various trades. His excellent grasp of the technical aspects of building in wood is especially evident in St. Paul's lofty post-and-beam interior (opp. page). Decoration, however, was left to a minimum; it was found only in the capitals of the posts supporting the roof, in bracketed rafter bracing, and in one or two simple Gothic details in the pews and the pulpit.

Overshadowing the altar, the pulpit at Metlakatla seemed to testify to Duncan's belief that the teaching aspect of the church should dominate the ritual aspects. In fact, the ultimate split between Duncan and the Church Missionary Society, which led to his moving to Annette Island, Alaska, along with six hundred Metlakatlans in 1887, was a result of his refusal to accept ordination and to allow the people Holy Communion.

Once Duncan had left Metlakatla, his place was taken by Bishop Ridley with whom he had argued so bitterly. Fourteen years after Duncan's departure, while the men were away salmon fishing in July 1901, a fire destroyed the church, the schools, and, indeed, most of the other buildings in the village. The bishop's papers, which burned with his house, would have been of great value for the history of the province. With the help of private donations from England and local gifts, a new church (this page) was constructed for the rebuilt village by October 1903. It was not as overpoweringly large as the old St. Paul's; its style was much less ponderous and more tranquil, and the roofline was unbroken by side gables.

Although the bell was at first mounted in a rough low tower, it was later installed in a tower which had been added to the side of the building. This church, too, was lost to fire, and now the Church Army Hall is used for services.

59

Methodist Church

PORT SIMPSON

Built 1874

Kate and Alfred Dudoward, two high-ranking Tsimshians converted in Victoria, established a mission at Port (Fort) Simpson in 1873. In 1874 they were joined by the Reverend Thomas Crosby, a missionary who had come to Victoria from Ontario in 1862 and who was largely responsible for founding nearly all of the Methodist missions on the north coast.

Port Simpson's buildings rivaled those of Metlakatla in size and surpassed them in quality of design. The church, for example, was 50 by 80 feet, with a tower 140 feet high. It was designed by Thomas Trounce, a Californian who arrived in Victoria in 1858 and drew the plans for the city's first police station and jail. Trounce was a prominent Methodist and extremely sympathetic toward the missions.

His design for the church at the Port Simpson mission called for an exaggeratedly high roof (probably to provide for an impressive vaulted interior), more than usually elaborate traceried windows, and a spire roof painted in contrasting bands of colour as in the later church at Kitwanga (p. 69). This grand building clearly influenced the designs not only of the Kitwanga Church, but also Christ Church, Kincolith (p. 61). In 1931 it was destroyed by fire.

As it was seen from the side at the turn of the century (bottom), the church had a home for girls to the left; beyond it, clearly seen from the sea (top 1881 photo), was the mission school.

Anglican Church

KINCOLITH

Built c. 1880

Kincolith was established as a new Christian village at the mouth of the Nass Straits in 1867 by Robert Tomlinson, Duncan's associate who later founded the village of Meanskinisht (p. 68). In 1883 Kincolith came under the charge of Archdeacon Collison, a missionary who accumulated a now famous collection of ethnographic materials during his years on the north coast.

The first church at Kincolith (top) was an unpretentious frame building with a short belfry. A larger church (not shown) dedicated in 1891 replaced it, but this building was destroyed in September 1893 by a fire which, according to a *Colonist* news report, *started in a house and destroyed almost half the village before it was brought under control*. About seventy-eight by thirty-seven feet, the building was valued at $7,650. Inflation reduces the impact of this figure, but an idea of how expensive this church was can be gained by comparing its cost with that of the church at Canoe Creek (p. 148) which was built in 1900 for $1,200.

In September 1900, Christ Church (bottom) was dedicated. It was an imposing building; its broad base and heavy looking asymmetrical towers gave it a very solid and stable appearance. The church bell hung in the structure to the right, the village's electrical generating plant.

A report written at the time of the dedication ceremony paid little attention to the building's exterior appearance and concentrated on the interior (top) which was decorated with cedar garlands for the opening.

The church, which consists of nave, aisles, tower, porches and vestry, holds about 500 people; the west front is flanked by two towers. The interior is of lofty proportions finished with red and yellow cedar; the east window is filled with stained glass; the choir stalls, reading desk and pulpit were made locally, the windows and doors being supplied by Mssrs. Muirhead & Mann. The lectern is of polished brass. In the spandrels of the chancel arch there are two conventional figures of angels, painted by one of the Natives. The furnishings of the sanctuary were supplied from Weiler Bros. Both Muirhead and Mann's sash-and-door factory and Weiler Brothers' furniture firm operated in Victoria.

Christ Church underwent refurbishing in 1961, when the exterior was changed considerably (bottom). New and broader siding replaced the old, and the decorative blind arcade was removed from beneath the triple-arched window of the main facade.

St. Andrew's Church

ANGLICAN (FORMERLY METHODIST)
GREENVILLE

c. 1900

A Methodist mission was established at the village of Lakalzap in the Nass Valley in 1877. It was renamed Greenville in honour of the early missionary, the Reverend A. E. Green. In 1904 the mission became Anglican because no Methodist missionary was available.

St. Andrew's Church is of a most uncommon design in its complete lack of Gothic detail. In some ways its features are Georgian: the palladian windows have pilasters and molded decorations at the top, and the upper portion of the tower, with its columns and ogee roof, is reminiscent of a Georgian garden pavilion.

During the oolichan run in March 1922, while most of the people were away fishing, a fire in Greenville destroyed St. Andrew's and about twenty-five houses. Disastrous fires of this kind were a constant threat to early wooden church buildings. To find more than one church burning down in the same village within a period of, say, ten years, was not unusual. Crude wood-burning stoves with few safety features heated both the churches and the surrounding homes. None of the building materials used was fire resistant, as are plaster, plasterboard, and asbestos. Major portions of Metlakatla (p. 57) and Kincolith (p. 61), as well as Greenville, were at one time or another burned, and the beautiful church at Kitwanga was nearly lost to a fire started in the roof by flying sparks from its own stovepipe. Robert Tomlinson, the early Anglican missionary, even taught himself brickmaking in order to build safe brick chimneys. Nonetheless, his church at Meanskinisht burned not long after his death in 1913.

Holy Trinity Church

ANGLICAN

AIYANSH

Dedicated 1895

In 1883, six years before Bishop Ridley ordained him, J. B. McCullagh arrived at the Indian village of Gitlakdamix on the Nass. His first efforts went towards building his log house before the onset of winter, but his records also show that he soon began his missionary work with determination. *My first attempts at preaching and teaching were very unwelcome and much resented by the Indians in general, and the medicine men in particular. It soon became evident to me that I must learn the language for myself and trust no longer in an interpreter. I gave eight solid hours a day for one year to the making of a Nishga-English grammar . . . and printed it on my typewriter.*

His effort was not wasted; after only two or three years, he and his converts began to build a Christian community three miles downstream from Gitlakdamix at a site named Aiyansh (the place of early blooming). By 1893 the village was sufficiently successful to establish a steam saw and planing mill, and by 1895, as a result, the settlement had changed from a scattered collection of log and traditional plank houses drawn up facing the river into a neat village of regular streets and frame houses with a handsome Anglican-Gothic church (this page). The circular spire on the church was the pride of the village and rose 106 feet from the ground above a buttressed tower with a crenellated cornice and pinnacles. The crenellated parapet and cornice were repeated in the short tower at the right of the facade.

Yet within fifteen years the people of Aiyansh had returned to their old village. Aiyansh was on lower ground and more prone to flooding than Gitlakdamix, and by 1910 most of the villagers at Gitlakdamix had become

64

Christians and welcomed the Aiyansh villagers back.

Abandoned, the church at Aiyansh lost its delicate spire in a gale. But in the winter of 1918, the villagers dragged the main part of the building to Gitlak-damix, where it became St. Peter's Church Army hall.

Paper and laths inside the hall now conceal the originally exposed rafters, but the boldly carved and decorated beams are still visible. The sophistication of the elaborate scissor-truss ceiling extended to other details of Holy Trinity's design which no longer survive, such as the furnishings and elaborate rood screen (bottom).

St. Bartholomew's Church

ANGLICAN

GITLAKDAMIX

Built 1910-15

St. Bartholomew's (top) was not
so elaborate architecturally as Holy
Trinity at Aiyansh (p. 64), but it had
a clerestory, a most unusual feature in a
wooden British Columbia building and
far more common in very large stone
churches. Its two rows of rectangular
clerestory windows must have added a
good deal of light to the interior.

Of all the Indian village churches in
British Columbia, this is the only one
known to incorporate a tower clock.
The Reverend Paul Mercer donated it
to the village in the early 1940s. It was
battery-operated. Although extremely
unusual, the clock seems a peculiarly
apt symbol for the way in which the
missionaries intended to alter Indian
society by teaching the kind of regula-
tion and order that an industrialized
culture required.

The church burned in March 1945.
When this unusual photograph was
taken, the bell tower had just caught
fire. Free-standing, it was typical of
those found in the Skeena and Nass
valleys and probably contained a bell so
large it could not safely be housed in a
tower attached to the church. The
power wires that ran in front of the
church show that Gitlakdamix at the
time of this fire was a well-to-do village.
Few interior villages had their own
electrical power generating plants in the
1940s, but both telephones and elec-
tricity had been in use in Gitlakdamix
since the 1920s.

66

The design of the present St. Bartholomew's (bottom) was obviously influenced by that of the previous building; again, the clerestory is a striking feature. It produces a lofty and light-filled interior (top). The finish and furnishings inside the church are mainly of unstained varnished plywood, and few details are particularly striking in their own right; but the overall effect is one of warmth and harmony reminiscent of older buildings.

Although relatively modern, this new church is included in this collection because it, too, now stands in a deserted village. Since it was built, the villagers have resettled at New Aiyansh, and Gitlakdamix is only a seasonal fishing camp.

Methodist Church

MEANSKINISHT

Built 1906-7

The Reverend Robert Tomlinson sided with William Duncan in Duncan's conflict with Bishop Ridley at Metlakatla. As a result, when Duncan had to leave the Church Missionary Society, Tomlinson chose to leave as well. He spent the winter of 1887-88 in Kitwanga and gathered a group of converts who moved with him down river to form an independent Christian village. Observation of the Sabbath there was so strict that the new village, named Meanskinisht, came to be nicknamed *The Holy City!* Riverboats were not even permitted to dock there to take on fuel on Sundays.

Tomlinson established a sawmill in the village to provide a financial base for the community, and lumber from Meanskinisht was used to construct the churches at Kitwanga (p. 69) and Hazelton (p. 76), as well as the village's own church (1908 photo). The building had twin crenellated fort-like towers topped by acutely pointed pinnacles and was cruciform in plan. It also appears to have had a number of attractive circular stained glass windows. Fire destroyed it at an unrecorded date.

The congregation in the village of Meanskinisht, or Cedarvale as it is now called, is no longer Methodist and presently attends services given by the Salvation Army in the old school building.

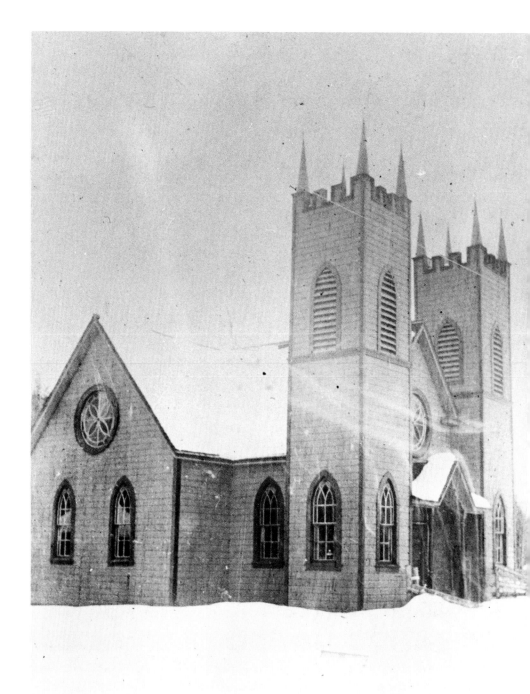

St. Paul's Church
ANGLICAN
KITWANGA
Built c. 1893

Shandilla, a broad flat on the river's edge with a grove of impressive cottonwood trees, was the site of the mission established near Kitwanga by the Reverend Alfred E. Price soon after his ordination by Bishop Ridley. After more of the people of Kitwanga became Christian, land in the village itself was given by the chiefs, and the mission was moved. St. Paul's Church, a school, and a vicarage were built during the 1890s. Only the church, one of the finest early wooden Anglican churches in the province, remains today.

Views of early buildings under construction are rare, but the progress of St. Paul's is exceptionally well documented; it is even possible to see the workmen installing boards used for sheathing (top). The spruce and cedar lumber for this building came by canoe from the early mill at Meanskinisht, about fifteen miles down river.

Building a church of the refinement and size of St. Paul's (thirty by sixty-seven feet) was a considerable undertaking, and it was not completely finished for some years. It stood for a year or two without much of its later trim and without its spire (below). When complete, the spire roof was painted with broad bands of dark and light colours in typical nineteenth-century style.

A long native tradition of woodworking on the north coast, combined with a strong interest on the part of the English Anglican missionaries in such industrial developments as sawmills, resulted in a speedy acceptance of new

woodworking tools. These tools were what made possible such work as the superb turned roof-corner finials of this building. And this kind of decoration often plays a major part in giving the north coast churches their distinctive character.

Handsome furnishings and a fine scissor-truss ceiling make the interior of St. Paul's a model of excellence in design and execution. Of the furnishings, the pulpit is especially outstanding as an exuberant combination of turned and sawn ornament. While its pedestal is vaguely Gothic in style, the pulpit proper is a strikingly original composition. By local tradition it is attributed to Joe Williams, a native of Kitwanga, who also worked on the church building. Adding to the richness of the darkly stained interior are four sanctuary windows. These are mid-nineteenth-century English stained glass and came in 1901 from an English church, where they were reputedly removed to make way for a memorial window to Queen Victoria. At the entrance, local red cedar has proved too soft for the butt hinges of the main doors, and at the top left one of the hinges has been incorrectly remounted.

St. Mark's Church

PENTECOSTAL (FORMERLY ANGLICAN)

KITWANCOOL

Built 1930

This church stands about fourteen miles north of Kitwanga. It was never entirely completed: for example, the lower left tower cornice, the bargeboards, and the siding of the lower towers are missing.

Although the construction work on this building was rough-and-ready, the design itself is practical and certainly not primitive or naive. It is, in fact, a variation of the early Anglican mission style found at its best in a church like St. Peter's, Hazelton (p. 76), especially in the crenellations and cornices on the tower.

Free-standing bell towers were common in the Skeena and Nass areas, where a very large bell was often a source of great pride among the congregation. The sheer weight of some bells made it dangerous to mount them in the church. Here, the tower seems to have been built to carry a large bell, but only a small simple one has been mounted.

The present Anglican church in Kitwancool is dedicated to St. Matthew. It is not shown because it was only recently reconstructed in Kitwancool after it had been moved there from its original site in Terrace. During the rebuilding, its original character was considerably modified.

United Church

Built c. 1930

Most of the best and most ambitious later Indian churches are to be found in villages like Kitseguecla in the Skeena and Nass Valleys. The most obvious source for the highly original design of this church is the triple-towered Salvation Army citadel at Glen Vowell (p. 78). Like many derivative buildings, however, this church is slightly less refined than its model. Nevertheless, the tower and cupolas make this building an excellent example of bold folk architecture, with their jagged opposing courses of cut shingles and massive roof finials. The vertically and diagonally running tongue-and-groove of the well-made arched doors act as a complement to the linear patterns of the siding and shingles.

Inside the church, two forms of pew, one a stiff design with a slight Anglican-Gothic flavour, the other an uncomfortable park bench type, were probably acquired at different times as the congregation grew, a common procedure. Boldly and simply designed, the original lectern is of cedar and typifies church furniture made locally after about 1910.

A series of sponge-painted wall and ceiling decorations of the kind popular at the turn of the century was the interior's most distinctive feature. At each end of the building, over the entry door and the sanctuary, were two large floral designs (opp. page) painted black on white and black on pink. They were connected by a narrow sponge-painted strip running along the middle of the ceiling and broken near the centre by a fret vent (bottom), which was itself painted black on red and black on white. These decorations were made by first cutting out and rounding the corners of the shapes to be applied. They were then painted with a base colour and given a mottled finish using a sponge dipped in a contrasting colour. When dry they were nailed to the ceiling.

This kind of painted decoration was popular in Indian and non-Indian churches in the early years of this century. But it has been removed nearly everywhere as part of modernization programmes. The example in this church was unusual, first, because it was made so late (after the 1920s) and, second, because it was not removed in 1976, when the building was remodeled. At that time, rooms were added to each side of the central tower, and the original tongue-and-groove doors were replaced by smooth plywood ones.

St. Peter's Church

ANGLICAN

HAZELTON

Built 1900

William Duncan's name is associated primarily with Metlakatla (p. 57), where his achievements among the Indians made him one of the most well-known Protestant missionaries in the English-speaking world. His powerful and domineering personality not only helped overcome difficulties and build Metlakatla but also occasionally created problems, especially when somebody, even an ecclesiastical superior, questioned his authority. When Bishop William Ridley arrived on his first visit to Duncan's village, a conflict quickly sprung up between the two men; it ended with Ridley spending the winter of 1880-81 on the Skeena River at Hazelton, rather than staying in Metlakatla and intensifying the dispute. During his stay, Ridley founded the Hazelton mission.

Modeled on the simple parish churches of rural England, St. Peter's Church has changed little since it was built looking out over the Skeena River (1911 photo). An English carpenter who later became a lay missionary at Kisgegas was in charge of construction, and his dominant tower with its attractive crenellation, cornice, and simple pinnacles shows the elegant, well-balanced design which is evident throughout the building.

Restrained taste and good craftsmanship combine in the arched tongue-and-groove paneled doors at the side of the tower and, in the interior, in the exposed scissor-truss ceiling. Walled throughout in vertical tongue-and-groove with an applied molded chair rail, the interior retains most of its

original furnishings, including the oil lamps (now electrified). The stained glass window is a memorial to the Reverend John Field, a missionary in Hazelton for thirty years early in this century. Its rich colours complement the dark stain finish of the walls and rafters.

Local craftsmen made the pews from native woods, but the oak pulpit was built in a factory and imported. It is far less ornate than the similarly shaped but handmade pulpit at Kitwanga (p. 69).

Salvation Army Citadel

Built c. 1900

During the winter of 1898, a number of
Kispiox villagers returned from the
coast to their homes professing to be
soldiers of the Salvation Army. Their
fellow villagers, who were Methodists,
forced them to leave, and they settled a
few miles down river from Kispiox.
Their new village was called Glen
Vowell, after the man who surveyed
their new homesite.

Salvation Army buildings are usually
very simple, but the citadel at Glen
Vowell was a notable exception. From
the first (top) it was an eccentric
structure, and the side doors in the
porch must have proved extremely awkward at times. By the 1940s (bottom)
the villagers had converted them into
windows, altered the porch roof, and let
a single door into the front. Odd as they
were, however, the square towers with
their lattice work openings and slightly
oriental-looking eaves were also highly
original examples of folk architecture.
They were removed in the 1950s but
restored in 1975, when transepts were
added.

The interior of the Glen Vowell hall
has been redesigned and walled in
vertical tongue-and-groove cedar, but
evidence uncovered during restoration
work indicates that it had an ochre-and-
brown grained, beaded tongue-and-
groove dado and horizontal tongue-and-
groove covered walls. Painted above the
stepped sanctuary platform was the
Salvation Army crest and the motto
Faith without Works is Dead.

There were two other Salvation Army
buildings (not shown) in the region.
The interior of the citadel at nearby
Hazelton was as austere as the one at
Glen Vowell, but Kitseguecla's building,
dating from the 1930s, had a large,
round, coloured glass window over the
sanctuary.

Methodist Church

Built 1901

In 1856, when William Pierce was born, his Scottish father was employed by the Hudson's Bay Company in Fort Simpson. His Indian mother died shortly after his birth, and he was raised by his Tsimshian grandparents. Under the influence of the Methodist missionary Thomas Crosby, he converted to Christianity, undertook a course of study in Victoria and then worked in the Skeena and Nass missions. In 1887 he was ordained at the first Methodist conference held in British Columbia, and in 1895 was transferred to Kispiox where he worked until he moved to Port Essington in 1910. His memoirs were eventually published under the title *Potlatch to Pulpit*.

When Pierce had been in Kispiox for six years, the villagers built a church characterized by a strongly divided tower and a bellcast roof covered with multicoloured shingles (top). This roof was topped by a delicate finial. In many ways this building was similar to the Salvation Army Hall at Glen Vowell p. 78), only a short distance away and built at about the same time. The line of the roof, the box cornice, the horizontal divisions, and the form of the tower were all more fully developed at Glen Vowell.

When this old church burned in 1945 only the robustly designed cedar font and several small pews were saved.

They continue in use at Pierce Memorial Church (bottom), which was built in 1949.

Even in 1975, when it was remodeled, this new church was not completely finished; but its pedimented window trim was especially attractive, and the spire, although weakly designed, was distinctive and interestingly fanciful. The remodeling involved enlarging the building and covering the walls with stucco, but the tower and spire were fortunately retained.

Southern Interior

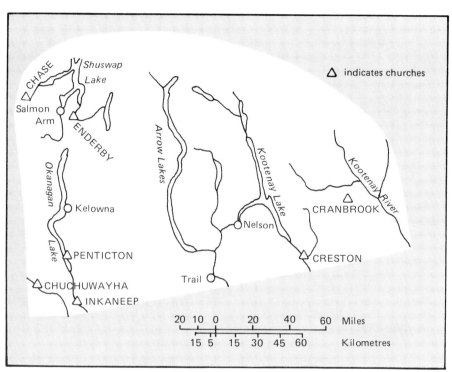

The west of this region consists of a level plateau carved by a number of deep river valleys, the largest of which are the Similkameen and the Okanagan. To the east lies the Kootenay district. This part of the region contains the Columbia mountain system, through which the Kootenay and Columbia rivers loop before continuing southward. The large Upper and Lower Arrow lakes and many smaller lakes lie in the mountain valleys.

Generally, annual precipitation in the western part of this region is lower than 50 cm. (20″), and in some areas it is less than 25 cm. (10″). Mean monthly temperatures on the plateau range from —12-—7° C (10-20° F) in the winter to 13 – 16° C (55 – 60° F) in the summer. In the valleys, mean temperatures are 6 – 8° C (10 – 15 F) higher, and in the Okanagan, particularly, summer maximums frequently reach 32° C (90° F).

Kootenay valleys experience three to five months of temperatures below freezing and in summer have mean monthly temperatures of around 16 – 20° C (60 – 68° F) in the valleys, slightly lower on the plateau. Precipitation is higher than in the west, averaging 50 – 75 cm. (20 – 30″) in the valleys and 100 – 125 cm. (40 – 50″) in the mountains. A large proportion of this precipitation (30 – 40 per cent in the valleys and 50 – 70 per cent in the mountains) comes in the form of winter snows.

Vegetation in the southern Okanagan is sparse, consisting mainly of sagebrush; elsewhere grassland covers both the plateau and the valleys. Mixed deciduous and coniferous forests occur in some areas of the Okanagan and

Similkameen Valleys. In the Kootenays, dry forests of Douglas fir and pine predominate, though deciduous trees such as birch and poplar line some valleys.

Four cultural subgroups live in the southwest Interior: the Thompson, Shuswap, Okanagan, and Lillooet people of the Interior Salish language group. All of these people originally lived in the summer in tepee-like, pole-framed structures covered with mats or skins. In winter they sheltered from the cold in pit houses dug into the ground. Social structure in Interior tribes was generally less rigidly organized than in coastal groups. They were a nomadic people, following game into the hills in the summer months and fishing from camps by the rivers in fall and winter. Since the 1890s, however, they have lived in more permanent villages, and many have gained employment in local industries.

The Kootenay Indian group which inhabited the eastern part of the region also traditionally lived in hide- or mat-covered tepees in summer, but in winter they built "A"-frame houses of poles covered with mats. Primarily a hunting people, they sometimes crossed the mountains to the east and, like the Indians of the Plains, hunted bison.

All the Indian churches in the southern Interior were built under Roman Catholic auspices. Some had regionally distinct features. In the Okanagan boldly decorated horizontal bands of wood often decorated church towers. Broad overhanging cornices and low four-sided spires with curved profiles helped to create a generally squat appearance. Kootenay church towers were noticeably different. Some had towers built in tiers, and their spires were either four-sided or polygonal, often with small gables.

St. Ann's Church

ROMAN CATHOLIC

CHUCHUWAYHA

Built c. 1910-11

When the present church of St. Ann with its high arched windows and small bellcast belfry was built on a hill above the village and the Similkameen River, the old church near the river became a house for occasional use by the itinerant priest. In 1898, after Father Le Jeune, one of the region's most famous priests, had been working in the Interior for sixteen years, he described some of the Roman Catholic missionary's special difficulties that made some form of residence in each village particularly welcome. *The same priest must attend to a district of several hundred miles of circuit, containing some 2,000 to 4,000 Indians, distributed in bands from 50 to 150 or 200* [the 1916 Reserve Commission lists Chuchuwayha's population as 32], *he cannot make very frequent visits to each place — three or four times a year at most. Were he to try and see them often, he could not, because most of the time the Indians would not be at home, but scattered over their fishing or hunting grounds, or engaged in other work which would keep them away from their camps.*

Holy Cross Church

ROMAN CATHOLIC

NESKAINLITH

n.d.

Situated on a hill above the southwest shore of Little Shuswap Lake and across the South Thompson River from Chase, the village of Neskainlith is built around the Church of the Holy Cross. Modern slab doors have replaced the original paneled ones, and sheet aluminum now covers the shingles of the large belfry's bellcast roof.

Well built in the first place, the church has been treated with care and attention. Over the years the exterior has changed very little.

Sacred Heart Church

ROMAN CATHOLIC

PENTICTON

Built 1910-11

Sacred Heart Church in Penticton is a well-finished, sturdy, but graceful building. It replaced a much smaller log building with a low pitched roof. The earlier building has been restored (without the belfry) and is now used as a cultural centre.

The Georgian revival of the early part of this century evidently influenced the pedimented entrance and the attractive arched, fan-shaped transom. Dentil cornices, the keystone trim of the round window and ventilator of the tower, and the arched windows are also consistent with this style. With its bell-cast roof, Sacred Heart is similar to the church at Moricetown (p. 162); both look heavy and lack fanciful details, but both are nonetheless attractive.

Now that its choir gallery has been removed, its walls resheathed in plywood, its vaulted ceiling hidden by a new and straightened one, and its old arcaded altar and simple reredos discarded, the interior at Penticton has lost all connection with its original design. Only the old leaded windows of coloured glass remain.

85

Roman Catholic Church

INKANEEP

Built c. 1885

Inkaneep is in the Okanagan Valley about six miles southeast of Oliver, and its village church is typical of those built throughout the valley in the 1880s and 1890s. Later but similar churches can still be seen at both Chuchuwayha (p. 83) and Penticton (p. 85).

A tower rising in a single stage and topped by a low, pyramidal spire is the hallmark of the regional style. The stringcourses above the entrance and below the highest tower openings emphasize the tower's generally squat appearance, but the double curves of these openings add considerably to the building's appeal.

At one time Inkaneep was the southernmost Oblate mission. Its church was called *the Divisional Church* because it marked the end of Oblate territory and the beginning of Jesuit territory in the United States.

St. Mary's Church
ROMAN CATHOLIC
ENDERBY

Built 1894

After 1890, the congregation at Enderby replaced their old log church with a new and larger frame building (1894 photograph with oddly retouched trees and bushes to each side of the church). The durable earlier structure continued to give good service as a band hall. The new building was distinguished by a very steep roof and a high tower. A simple sawtooth cornice below double pointed openings in the spire provided relief detail.

In 1916 lightning struck the tower and the church burned. The bell fell from the tower and, although cracked, was installed in the present church (below), where it is still used today. The new church itself is a neat plain building with an attractive bellcast belfry roof and triple-arched windows above the entrance porch.

In the earlier interior, the board-and-batten walls were stained and varnished, and the ceiling was painted a light colour. The rich dark stain provided a strong contrast with the church's elaborately gilded imported altar. When this 1894 photograph was taken, Easter celebrations were in progress, as the paschal candle to the left indicates.

St. Peter's Church

ROMAN CATHOLIC
LOWER KOOTENAY

Built 1903

Father Nicholas Coccola supervised the
construction of this attractively proportioned church on a site just south of
Creston. The building overlooks the
Kootenay River Valley. The tower,
built in distinct tiers, and the four-sided
spire decorated with small gables are
features typical of many churches in
both Indian and non-Indian settlements
in the Kootenays. Similar churches still
stand in Moyie, Greenwood, and Fort
Steele.

The interior of this church has been
renovated, and the original barrel-vault
is now covered by a low, flat false
ceiling.

Father Coccola seems to have had a
good design sense, judging by the buildings constructed in his parishes. It was
while he was stationed at Necoslie that
the spire of Our Lady of Good Hope
(p. 173) was built, and he probably
participated in the final design for St.
Eugene's at Cranbrook (p. 90).

St. Eugene's Church

ROMAN CATHOLIC

CRANBROOK

Built 1897

St. Eugene's is the finest late Victorian wooden church remaining in British Columbia. It was built in the late 1890s after Father Nicholas Coccola had urged the villagers to try mineral prospecting in an effort to make money to build a new and badly needed church. In 1893 the prospecting villagers discovered what became the St. Eugene silver, lead, and zinc mine, and it was with the proceeds from the mine's sale to the mining company which later became Cominco, that they built not only St. Eugene's but also another church in nearby Moyie.

Like Our Lady of the Rosary at Sechelt (p. 34), this church was professionally designed, and it was built largely by trained carpenters. The facade is a carefully considered composition; plain and fret borders divide it into small areas and emphasize a sense of vertical movement which is reinforced by the pinnacles and buttresses at each corner. No surviving example matches the delicacy of conception and workmanship found in such details as the scalloped louvres, blind windows, and cut shingles. The facade is not today quite as it was when built; a statue of St. Eugène de Mazenod, the patron of the mission and the founder of the Oblate order, originally stood on the short pedestal at the centre of the base of the spire, below the spire gable.

91

From the side the church's fine brick chimneys can be seen. More often a simple iron stovepipe conducted the smoke outside. Also revealed, towards the rear of the building, is an odd architectural inconsistency where the sanctuary window breaks the eave of the sacristy roof.

A few of the interior details justify Father Coccola's calling St. Eugene's a *gothic* church — the arch and clustered columns on either side of the sanctuary, the three niches for statues, the sanctuary door pediment decoration, and, of course, the standard pointed windows. But the appeal of the interior comes not so much from Gothic details as from balance and proportion, especially in the way the smaller board-and-batten areas have been delineated. Similarly, the interior doors throughout the building faithfully echo the design and workmanship of the main entrance.

92

The altar, too, is particularly attractive. Such details as the tabernacle's capitals and spandrels and those of the canopy above it must have been carved by a skilled cabinet maker. The mass-produced plaster bas relief of the Last Supper that he has incorporated in the altar is used in the same way in the church at Kamloops (p. 107) and in other non-Indian churches.

The confessional is at the opposite
end of the interior, set below and to the
right of the choir gallery with its Gothic
quatrefoil decorated rail. It is similar to
the confessional at Skookumchuck (p.
117), but it is less flamboyant, in
keeping with the design of this building.

Thompson-Nicola

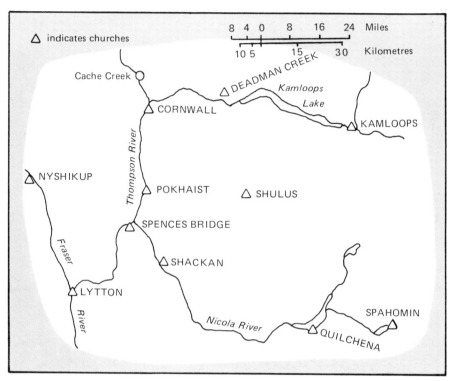

The Nicola River flows into the Thompson River at Spences Bridge, while the Thompson River enters the Fraser River at Lytton. Like the Okanagan and Similkameen rivers, they flow through valleys cut into the Interior plateau.

Mean temperatures in the region are comparable to those elsewhere in the southern Interior: around —8° C (17° F) in winter, 16° C (60° F) in the summer. Mean temperatures are slightly higher in summer in the valleys. As in the Okanagan, summer maximums are often higher than 27° C (80° F). The Thompson Valley is slightly drier than the Nicola Valley, where precipitation exceeds 50 cm. (20″) per year.

Open forests of yellow pine and Douglas fir cover the region's hills, and impressive stands of cottonwood line some riverbanks and lakeshores. These valleys were populated by the Thompson, Shuswap, and Okanagan sub-groups of the Interior Salish language group. Like the other bands of the Interior, the natives of this region trapped, fished, and hunted, moving their camps from valleys to hills in search of food. In summer they lived in mat- or skin-covered tepees, and in the cold winter months their shelters were pit-houses entered by means of a central ladder. Nowadays, many of the Indian people of this region work on the large cattle ranches which have been developed over the last century.

Because these bands were smaller and poorer than most coastal groups, both Roman Catholic Oblate and Anglican churches in the region were not generally elaborate. Many Anglican buildings lacked chancels and had simple barrel-vaulted ceilings rather than the open timber roofs found in north coast Anglican churches. Roman Catholic buildings lacked distinct regional characteristics. They formed a diverse group ranging from the elegantly simple church at Quilchena to the awkward but appealing building at Spahomin.

St. Augustine's Church

ANGLICAN

NYSHIKUP

n.d.

Shingles are rarely seen as wall covering in early British Columbia Indian village churches, and seldom are churches as small and simple as St. Augustine's at Nyshikup, high above the Fraser River near Lillooet. In the mind of the passer-by, this building may perfectly fit a simple stereotype of the pioneer church built in the 1860s, but St. Augustine's was actually built after 1914. Very few of the first generation of British Columbia churches have survived.

Four poles, one at each corner, are braced and covered with shingles to create the tower. Below, a measure of dignity is given by the arched entrance leading to the heavy paneled doors, which probably came from an earlier building. This church is now used as a storage shed.

Sts. Mary and Paul Church

ANGLICAN

LYTTON

Rededicated 1937

The present church at Lytton (top), set against the pine-covered hills above the junction of the Thompson and Fraser Rivers, is a memorial to Archdeacon Richard Small. From 1897 until his death in 1909, he was superintendent of the Indian missions in the diocese of New Westminster. Lytton was his home mission, and the earlier church there became known as the *Cathedral Church of the Thompson Indians*.

This old church (bottom) was rebuilt in the mid 1930s, and it was during this remodeling that the porch was moved from the side to the end of the nave and Small's memorial window was installed. Designed in the Tudor style fashionable in houses in the 1930s, the window was made in Vancouver. Other alterations dating from the same period included changing the trim, adding the gable overhang and simple buttresses, and converting the gable form of the belfry roof into its present steep bellcast shape.

The elaborately beamed lych gate is a feature typical of Anglican churchyards. Traditionally, it was the sheltered point at which the coffin was set down at a funeral to await the clergyman's arrival.

Church of St. Michael and All Angels

ANGLICAN

SPENCES BRIDGE

Built c. 1906

Every house was destroyed [by the land-slide], *thousands of tons of earth were piled up on what had been the site of the village, and the remnants of the buildings, many of them log houses, were swept into one corner against the bank under whose shelter* [the village] *stood. So complete was the destruction that not two boards, nor two logs held together with the one exception of the roof of the church, which, carried far from its original site, surmounted the debris and wreckage* (Inland Sentinel, 15 August 1905).

The Indian village and church at Spences Bridge were completely destroyed in this landslide of 13 August 1905. A new village and church were begun shortly after on higher ground.

Shakes cover the original cove siding and now overpower this simple building, whose octagonal tower roof has been mounted on the square tower in an extremely original manner. The overall effect is, when combined with the narrowness of the tower itself and the shake siding, unusual in British Columbia. The small squat openings beneath the tower roof are almost the only features of this building which refer to any recognizable church style.

In the interior, a boldly designed altar rail stands out against the austere undecorated tongue-and-groove walls and ceiling. The slab door to the left of the altar and the vestry to which it leads are not original.

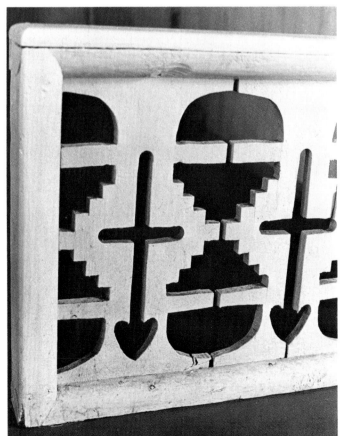

St. Aidan's Church

ANGLICAN

POKHAIST

n.d.

Built on a flat above the east bank of the Thompson at the foot of a large rock slide and craggy bluff, the little church at Pokhaist is dwarfed by its lonely setting. Only the poor, narrow, winding road from Spences Bridge and the equally poor and longer road from Ashcroft make Pokhaist accessible by automobile. In a less grand setting, St. Aidan's would likely be overlooked, but because of its splendid isolation it has become a landmark for travelers passing on the highway on the other side of the river.

Everything about the church is plain, except for a hint of the Gothic style in the pointed windows and the shallow pointed arch above the four-panel door. The interior is sheathed in unstained tongue-and-groove cedar.

Church of St. John at the
Latin Gate

ANGLICAN

CORNWALL

Built 1880-91

The village of Cornwall near Ashcroft is built on the broad bench above the Thompson River very near the old roadhouse called Ashcroft Manor. Sometime between 1880 and 1891 the Cornwall brothers, one of whom later became lieutenant-governor of British Columbia, financed the building of the church as part of an agreement for transferring ownership of a piece of land.

Small and with a lower pitched roof than most, the church is finely built: its logs are squared, and the corners are precisely dovetailed. The solid old four-panel door, whose sill is now rotting, is given a touch of dignity by the addition of a low pediment above. It is a very basic building which, fitted with pointed windows and a small belfry, has become a church. There is nothing in its plan to distinguish it from a pioneer school or cabin.

Tongue-and-groove cedar lines the plain but well-finished interior. The cedar is darkened with age except where an earlier and larger drapery behind the altar covered it. The cedar altar is decorated with a blind arcade of pointed arches and trefoils. Its central panel carries an applied fret cross formed from stylized lilies.

St. Philip's Church

ANGLICAN

SHACKAN

Built c. 1915

In the unusual stepped design of its porch and tower, the church at Shackan resembles St. Aidan's, Pokhaist (p. 101), although their tower openings, roof and window shapes, and general proportions are quite different. At this church, the windows are very simply trimmed; their pediments add a touch of grace to the hewn log walls, which are precisely dovetailed at each corner. The wall cracks have never been chinked, but the interior finish of tongue-and-groove boards makes the building effectively weathertight.

From the prayer desk to the varnished pine pews, the furnishings are very plain. A sheet of prefinished birch plywood in place of altar drapery appears alien and strange in a setting of tongue-and-groove walls. This kind of panel is one of the most common materials used to modernize rural church interiors, and when it is used throughout a building, the character of the interior is completely destroyed.

St. Mary's Church

ROMAN CATHOLIC

DEADMAN CREEK

Built c. 1910

Four years after thieves removed the leaded glass windows from this church in 1973, the courts were still holding the windows as evidence. They were essentially the only ornaments in an otherwise plain cove-sided building, whose interior is covered with embossed sheet iron like that at Necoslie (p. 173).

St. Joseph's Church

ROMAN CATHOLIC

KAMLOOPS

Built 1900

Situated on a broad flat at the junction of the North and South Thompson Rivers, the present Kamloops reserve church, St. Joseph's (top), once stood in the centre of the old village (bottom), but the layout of the village has changed around it. The church now stands on its own in a very widely scattered group of houses.

Father Jean-Marie Le Jeune (shown kneeling, centre, in the undated archival photograph over page) developed a system of easily learned shorthand for some Indian languages and used it in a newspaper he published called the *Kamloops WaWa*. His many notes of his experiences in the southern Interior form a valuable record of the Roman Catholic missionary's life at the turn of the century. He witnessed various stages of St. Joseph's construction.

The Indians worked on their church between 30th of October and the 10th of November 1900. The old log church [shown covered with cove siding behind congregation] has been torn down, and a new frame structure put in its place. The dimensions are 75 feet from the front door to the end of the sanctuary and there is a transept 50 feet by 20. The walls are 16 feet high. The services of a good carpenter were secured, and the Indians helped as much as they could; at times there were more than 50 working together. By the 10th of November the church was finished outside, the windows and doors put in their places, and the ceiling completed inside. Here we have to take a rest, for the Indians do not want to miss their fall hunt of deer for meat, and everyone takes a five weeks licence. About the 16th of December they will be all around again and it will take only a few days to complete the work inside.

The church was blessed, as anticipated, on the Sunday before Christmas 1900.

Although Father Le Jeune reports that the old log church was torn down, it was not entirely demolished. The tower was retained and incorporated into the new building. Visually it made a strong vertical impact in the facade of the original log building, but the new facade loses this effect because the new walls are higher and because the front of the tower is flush with the front of the facade. The spire thus becomes an overlarge belfry.

Two stock sashes next to each other above the entrance make an unusual transom. At the foot of each arch and in the other windows of the facade, corner blocks have been drilled with four holes to create a slightly spare or stark decorative effect; turned rosettes as at Seton Portage (p. 125) were the usual choice for such decoration. The appearance of the main entrance in the facade has been marred by the modern slab doors which replace the original four-panel ones.

Reconstruction of the kind at St. Joseph's can create eccentricities not only in the exterior of the building but also in the interior. Here, the new ceiling cuts off the top of the bull's eye window which belonged to the original tower.

The stations of the cross ranked along both side walls at Kamloops are unusual. Stations of the cross in rural Roman Catholic churches in British Columbia are almost invariably framed prints, usually chromolithographs. These plaster ones came from a church supply house, probably the one which provided the polychrome plaster relief of the Last Supper incorporated in the altar.

Massive, but fancifully designed, this altar is unlike any of the known factory-built examples. Although it was made by a craftsman of considerable skill, the naive style of its painted and gilded cupolas and of the fret decoration applied to the tabernacle door indicate that it was probably manufactured locally. Factory-made applied motifs are always machine stamped and give the effect of carving. But here the craftsman has had to draw his design on a piece of wood, cut it out, and apply it to the surface, a far more time-consuming operation.

Church of the Immaculate Conception

ROMAN CATHOLIC

SHULUS

Built 1892-93

In 1892, according to one of Father Le Jeune's notes, timber had already been cut and a fund was being started to complete construction of this church at Shulus. By 1893 the church (top) was probably finished. Corrugated metal now covers the original shingles, and the otherwise plain church gains most of its appeal from the ogee arches of the drum openings, a stylized fret cross, and different patterns of cut shingle on the spire roof.

Rural church windows in British Columbia were almost always manufactured in urban sash-and-door factories and followed patterns fashionable at the time. Towards the end of the nineteenth century, fashion seems to have shifted away from narrow and emphatically vertical proportions typical of slightly earlier buildings (see pp. 134, 90) to the wider form seen in this church.

Shulus is also served by a small Anglican church, All Saints (bottom), which originally had a slightly Georgian appearance. Its character has been completely changed by the recent addition of a prominent belfry, but one or two details are successful. Especially noteworthy is the cornice at the corners of the roof, where the corner capping is made to imitate pier capitals.

Church of Our Lady of Lourdes

ROMAN CATHOLIC

QUILCHENA

Dedicated 1893

Church building projects in rural areas like Quilchena were frequently co-operative ventures, and they relied on volunteers to work alongside paid experts, who would usually supervise. According to parish records in Kam-loops, the experts involved at Quilchena were A. H. Owen assisted by Tom Hunter and Joe Smollett. Joseph Guichon, one of the most prominent ranchers in the upper Nicola Valley, donated the lumber.

Their cooperation resulted in a simple but handsome building both well con-ceived and professionally executed. The extension with rectangular windows and the lean-to were not part of the original building; they were added in preparation for a visit by Bishop Augus-tine Dontenwill in 1902, shortly after he succeeded Bishop Durieu.

Apart from these additions, the exterior is in largely original condition, including the drilled and cut trim at the edge of the bellcast spire roof and the molded capitals of the arcaded spire drum. The interior, however, has been extensively modernized with plywood sheathing, and the old altar has been removed. A little information about the impression it originally created survives in Father Le Jeune's account of the opening. He refers to *a magnificent statue of Our Lady of Lourdes, five feet high ... placed in an azure-coloured niche, in the centre of a background of red drapery above the altar.*

One of the entrances at the base of the tower is no longer used; however, the doors — of an exceptionally attrac-tive herringbone design — remain, although they are now structurally weak and broken.

112

St. Nicholas's Church

ROMAN CATHOLIC

SPAHOMIN

Dedicated 1889

Although much simpler, St. Nicholas's Church recalls the church torn down at Kamloops in 1900 (p. 108). It has the same disproportionately large tower centred in the facade, and the main portion of the building is of log, covered with cove siding.

Father Le Jeune was involved in constructing both churches. But he was noted for being an inexpert designer and carpenter and probably played only a small role in the design and building at Kamloops. However, his serious lack of design sense perhaps explains why the transom window has been positioned in this tower as if floating above the door. The peculiar little braces at the base of the tower seem to betray the same lack of expertise. To place vertical bars in the tower's openings is equally eccentric.

Inside the church, the cornice moldings which hide the ends of the tongue-and-groove boards are especially fine, and the door is an excellent board-and-batten example complete with old cast-iron hinges. Board-and-batten is the most common and straightforward construction method for doors in rural buildings; ordinary lumber can be used with nails to minimize the need for complex joinery. True paneled doors require much more time and skill, and more elaborate tools, because genuine panels are actually let into a flat surface by means of complicated joining techniques. Here, the front of the door remains completely undecorated.

The main altar has disappeared, but the false-panel decoration of the two side altars was probably repeated on its front at least. So-called false panels imitate true paneling by using boards and strips of molding applied to a wide board.

Lillooet-Brigade Trail

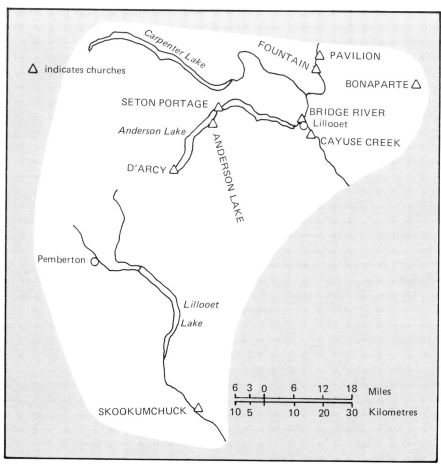

This isolated region lies between Harrison Lake and Lillooet, to the west of the Thompson-Nicola region and south of the Cariboo-Chilcotin. It is an area of numerous small lakes and valleys cut by rivers like the Lillooet itself.

Protected by the coastal mountains from damp Pacific air, the west of the region receives only light precipitation by coastal standards — 65–90 cm. (25″–35″) annually — and temperatures range from winter means of around —7° C (20° F) to summer means near 18° C (65° F). Game is abundant in the mixed forests of the hills and valley bottoms.

Of all the Interior Salish subgroups in the region at the time of initial missionary activity, the Lillooet people had had the most extensive contact with the coast and absorbed more characteristics of coastal culture. Their winter ceremonies in particular were more extensively developed than those of other Interior bands. Farther inland, near Pavilion and Bonaparte, the region was inhabited by bands belonging to the Shuswap culture group, whose social organization followed the pattern of the other nomadic Interior tribes.

The church buildings of this region — all Roman Catholic — were frequently similar to the ambitiously designed Gothic churches built on the southern coast and in the Fraser Valley. Church interiors in the Lillooet Valley and at Anderson Lake were particularly rich and elaborate, with ornate altars, chancel rails, and reredoses. Ceilings, too, throughout the area still present a variety of angular and curved forms.

Church of the Holy Cross

ROMAN CATHOLIC

SKOOKUMCHUCK

Built 1905-6

A great deal of the power of the splendid Gothic church at Skookumchuck lies in its location. It is totally unexpected, a cathedral in the wilderness accessible only by a rough logging road. The mission itself was established in 1861, and the present church is the third built on or near the site of the first. Of all the early church buildings remaining in British Columbia, only one or two, such as St. Eugene's, Cranbrook (p. 90), and St. Paul's, Kitwanga (p. 69), can compare with it in terms of elaborate decoration.

The triple-spired facade is made particularly imposing by the unbroken lines of the octagonal towers thrusting strongly upward. These spires were once topped by fret crosses nearly five feet high, one of which is preserved inside the building. The many windows mounted in each tower contribute further to an overall impression of grandeur.

Scalloped bargeboards create the effect of lace along both the main facade gable and the row of smaller gables around each spire drum. Pairs of brackets with a scroll form decorate the tower cornices below the drum; and above it, slender corner capping dominates the spire decoration. The courses of scalloped and pointed shingles add a subtle variation in texture. The arched transom of the entrance, with its pair of paneled and glazed doors, echoes elements of the round or rose windows in the facade.

Even the complex and elaborate facade, however, is hardly adequate preparation for the ornate interior. The display of applied decoration on the ceiling above the sanctuary is especially noteworthy. Although it owes much to the influence of the Gothic Revival, it is also very inventive.

Skookumchuck's altar is slightly higher than that at St. Joseph's, Kamloops (p. 109), but it is on the same scale. The effect here is infinitely lighter; a graceful colonnade breaks up the lines of the solid altar front.

Among the mass of decoration of the reredos and above the plaster statue of the sacred heart is a dove representing the Holy Ghost. This dove is the only known early example of locally executed sculpture in any of the rural churches. Plaster statues were so readily available by the later nineteenth century, and the tradition of sculpture was so undeveloped among the Indians of the Interior, that local native sculpture on Christian themes did not spring up there as it had in the earlier Spanish missions in New Mexico and further south. Local woodwork, as opposed to sculpture, however, is evident everywhere in British Columbia Indian churches. Below the reredos, for example, the tabernacle mixes design motifs in a manner typical of local work: the arch surrounding the door has a slight Romanesque flavour, but the design of the cross is highly original.

Even the details of the pews are exceptional, and the combination of turned wood and carved decoration is very unusual indeed. Turned decoration, which requires much less time and skill, is found more frequently than carving. Here, the reeded central section and the carved octagonal knob finials are outstanding. The confes-

sionals on each side of the main door under the choir are crowned with pinnacles, crocketted gables, rows of bosses, and scrolled motifs like those above the arcaded door opening.

Chapel, St. Ann's Convent
New Westminster B.C. 1878

Although the decoration of the sanctuary at Skookumchuck is very elaborate, it is not without precedent. Built in 1878, the chapel of St. Ann's convent in New Westminster (top) had a similar set of Gothic decorations. The style was less fully developed, but it conveyed the same general impression, especially in its colonnaded altar front at the right and the large central ceiling rosette of plaster, from which the main sanctuary lamp hung.

The sanctuary lamp at Skookumchuck hangs from a ceiling rosette, but this one is made of fret and turned wood. It is set in a herringbone design border of tongue-and-groove boards.

Holy Rosary Church

ROMAN CATHOLIC

D'ARCY

Built c. 1900

D'Arcy is a small village on the rail line in the Mount Currie area. Its homes cluster round the church, which is a simpler version of the one at Anderson Lake (p. 122). Still in use, the little building looks odd now that the octagonal spire with its band of pointed shingles has settled part way into the tower.

The most notable features of the exterior are the brackets under the eaves. Although these are plainly cut, together with the toothy border of shingles on the spire, they add charm to an otherwise plain exterior.

Lined with horizontal boards, the interior, too, is more than usually plain. Its statues are of unglazed porcelain, or parian ware, in place of the more usual polychromed plaster. A print of the Last Supper decorates the altar, which has a Gothic style reredos. The fact that plywood is used in the altar suggests that it is either a recent replacement or an earlier altar rebuilt. It has been stained and varnished to match the simple dado of vertical boards.

To the rear, the choir gallery rail repeats the simple chamfered design of the altar rail.

Roman Catholic Church

ANDERSON LAKE

Built c. 1895

Total transformation of the Indians' lifestyle was one of the prime objectives of the missionaries who came to British Columbia. Their churches were symbols of the way of life that they brought with them from Europe and eastern Canada and hoped to impose on the Indians. As a consequence, these buildings contain few material expressions of Indian culture.

Nevertheless, a few details are more likely to be found in Indian churches than elsewhere. Strong, bright colours are often used for trim and furnishings: at Pavilion the pews are mustard yellow (p. 132); the red exterior trim at Tachie (p. 168) is quite striking; and the ceiling of the old church at Old Fort Babine (p. 164) is painted in large distinct blocks of varied colour.

From the exterior, this church at the north end of Anderson Lake is not outstanding, although the little octagonal spire has bands of scalloped and pointed shingles above its simple arched drum. The interior, however, contains a profusion of elaborate fretwork based on Indian folk motifs unmatched in any other building.

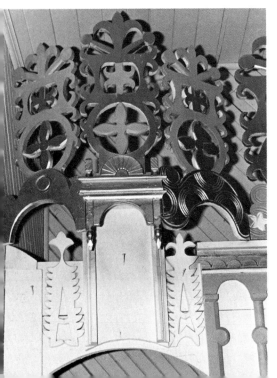

Of all the locally made altars this is the most original and the most delightful. Except for the monogram, the Gothic arches, and the shell in the lunette at the centre of the base, its decoration involves no direct borrowing from standard examples. Though of a different design, the choir rail and the altar rail both have the same lacelike appearance. At the same time, a sense of movement is conveyed by the tongue-and-groove boards arranged in sections on the bias in opposition to each other. The choir supports are carved from large timbers and decorated with applied molding at their capitals.

St. Mary's Church

ROMAN CATHOLIC

SETON PORTAGE

n.d.

The village of Seton Portage lies at the west end of Seton Lake; a narrow gravel road runs over the mountains to connect it with Lillooet. When the foundations of the village's small hewn log church had deteriorated badly and made the building unusable, demolition plans were prepared. But the church had become so essential a part of community life that the older people wanted it to remain as long as it could stand.

The logs are exposed on the sides and rear of the church; only the facade and the porch, which is a frame structure, have cove siding. Two further details of the exterior are particularly attractive: the little belfry with its cut shingle roof and the handmade door. The builder has made the board-and-batten door appear paneled by using two very wide boards; the design is not traditional — a chamfered panel is centred in each of two full-length, arched, flat panels.

In remote areas inventiveness is essential, and available materials must be made suitable. The transom window above the entrance door has been made by installing the lower half of a double-hung sash on its side (the wider bottom member is at the right), and an iron bedstead to the right of the building acts as a gate.

The small structure to the rear of the church was used by the priest during his periodic visits to the village, at a time when the area he covered in the Interior could be enormous. While Father Adrien G. Morice, the pioneer anthropologist, was working at the Stuart Lake Mission (Necoslie) he wrote, *from May 13th to September 28th, 1895, I spent only a week and a half at home. During my travels I suppose I covered at least 1900 miles on foot, by canoe and on horse back.*

Inside St. Mary's, arched partition openings on each side of the altar resemble those at nearby Anderson Lake (p. 122). Behind them and the altar, such things as vestments used to be stored, and the partition also conceals the door leading to the priest's cabin. Despite these similarities to the Anderson Lake church, there is none of that building's extraordinary sawn ornament in this interior. The altar front is plain with only a wide border of molding, and the tabernacle carries strange crude decoration reminiscent of that found on medieval stone buildings. While the altar rail is almost identical to the rail at Anderson Lake, finials decorate each end of this one where it meets the wall. Their design is an original synthesis of common folk art motifs: heart, flower, arrow, and circle.

An unusual combination of moldings and corner blocks trims the window around the incorrectly installed sashes (the lower sash has been installed upside down at the top, and the upper one upside down at the bottom). There has also been some difficulty in making the frame fit the arched portion of the sash.

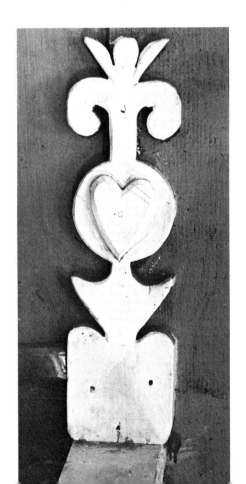

St. James's Church
ROMAN CATHOLIC
BRIDGE RIVER

Blessed 1912

In 1912, Bishop Alexander MacDonald, bishop of Victoria, wrote, *The following day* [21 June] *we bless the new church* [at Bridge River] *and erect Stations of the Cross. The houses* [of the village] *are built on a level plot of ground some way up the mountain. It forms what is known in this country as a 'bench', and bears about the same relation to the rest of the hill as a bracket does to a wall. The spot is a most picturesque one, overlooking Bridge River and the Fraser where they meet. Here both streams pass tumultuously through canyons, and the roar of their rushing waters is still in my ears. Water has to be 'packed' up hither from the river, some three quarters of a mile away, by a steep road or trail.*

St. James's was less elaborate than the neighbouring church at Fountain (p. 130), although its modest spire had a certain appeal. Attractive double-arched louvred openings rose above the bracketed cornices, and the shingles of the spire roof were cut with unusual reversed scalloping. The applied lozenge decoration in the apex of each gable was a further refinement.

The building stood in a deserted village until a brush fire destroyed it in the late 1960s. Before the fire, the effects of abandonment were evident. In the interior, statues and other decorations had disappeared; the tabernacle, prayer desk, and other remaining furnishings were scattered.

Another brush fire destroyed the nearby Lillooet church and the native village of Lillooet itself a few years later in 1971.

127

St. Andrew's Church

ROMAN CATHOLIC

CAYUSE CREEK

n.d.

It is not certain that this small log church, set halfway down the wall of the Fraser Valley near Lillooet, was actually built between 1860 and 1890, but its method of building certainly belongs to that generation. Because of its present condition, it provides an ideal illustration of basic hewn log construction techniques.

Frequently, no foundations are used for log buildings of this kind: the first log is simply laid directly on the ground. When foundations are necessary, as on the slope at Cornwall (p. 102), they are of fieldstone or blocks of wood.

Except in very simple buildings, when logs may be left round, the logs are flattened and then dovetailed at each end — usually with a saw and hand ax. They can then be interlocked at the corners of the structure. Windows and door frames are pegged or nailed to the ends of shorter logs where openings are required. The frames both tie the logs together and receive the sashes and doors. Once the walls are as high as needed, the roof is constructed like that of any frame building. Gaps between the logs are filled first with poles, if the gap is large, and then with mortar. If mortar is not available, straw and mud or moss and mud are used.

If siding is to be added, battens must be nailed on to provide a sufficiently uniform nailing surface for the horizontal boards, and the dovetailed corners must be trimmed flush. At Cayuse Creek, the right but not the left rear corner has been trimmed; only the facade and one wall have cove siding.

Roman Catholic Church

FOUNTAIN

Built c. 1890-1900

Built on an ambitious scale, this cruciform church at Fountain, near Lillooet, had a spire design based on those of Our Lady of the Rosary, Sechelt (p. 34). In contrast to the spire at nearby Bonaparte (p. 134), which is a simplified copy of the Sechelt model, this spire was an elaborate adaptation of it. It sat atop a plain cove-sided tower with a neat bracketed cornice and rounded windows.

Simple hewn log buildings probably made up the first village on the site in the 1860s. Before then, the people of this region had been nomadic. But the large numbers of newcomers drawn into the area by the rush for gold disrupted the Indians' traditional patterns of behaviour, and outbreaks of smallpox added to their difficulties. At the same time, the Roman Catholic missionaries were especially active along the Fraser Valley and in the Interior.

The Indians welcomed the new order which these missionaries offered them. Between the 1860s and the turn of the century, the missions prospered; dominant and confident buildings like the church at Fountain were built to accommodate the expected future growth of an expanding congregation. But often the increase in numbers failed to continue, and the history of many of the more impressive and complicated churches follows the same pattern as that of this building. By the 1950s it had become too great a drain on the resources of the congregation, and it was razed to the ground. Its place was taken by a simple, smaller, more utilitarian frame structure which incorporated some of the windows and pews, fragments of the altar reredos, the tabernacle, the stations of the cross, and the statues from the demolished building.

Two details of the pews show well
how mass-produced imported furniture
influenced local work. A hand-carved
applied arch motif at the end of the
pews is clearly an adaptation of the pew
decoration at Stony Creek (p. 178),
which was made in a factory.
Similarly, the carved stars in this church
are local handmade variations on
Stony Creek's factory-made turned
rosettes. At Bonaparte (p. 134), the
motif on the pews is an even more
simplified imitation of the same design.

Holy Trinity Church

ROMAN CATHOLIC

PAVILION

Built c. 1890-1910

Pavilion is in the Cache Creek/Clinton area, and its church, Holy Trinity, has a spire which rivals in its own way the ones at nearby Bonaparte (p. 134) and Fountain (p. 130). It derives its delicate elegance from the combination of scalloped shingles and the fine fret ornament concentrated in its eaves and in the cross above.

Great improvements in woodworking tools took place during the industrial revolution, and in the mid-nineteenth century, the bandsaw was invented. With these developments came the use, in nearly all wooden buildings, of very fanciful and elaborate sawn wood ornament, whose contribution to the overall appearance of wooden rural churches was enormous. It could be used virtually everywhere: in roof cresting, spire trim, cornice brackets, porch brackets, choir rails, or in the kind of scrolled trim beneath the windows at Pavilion, outside and in.

Although the interior at Pavilion is generally undistinguished, the white and blue altar, made locally, shows restraint in its use of rather heavy, even coarse, ornament. Its original character is very much changed by the addition of a tulip shaped backboard and the removal of its

stepped platform, whose outline is
visible on the back wall. The cloverleaf
decoration on the altar's central panel
is especially appropriate: it represents
the Holy Trinity, to whom the building
is dedicated.

By the turn of the century the church
had probably already acquired all three
types of the pews now in use, and in the
view to the rear of this interior, only the
light bulb and cord break the illusion of
a scene from the early 1900s. Originally
an oil lamp would have hung from the
attractive ceiling medallion.

133

St. Louis's Church

ROMAN CATHOLIC

BONAPARTE

Built 1890

Indians from Bonaparte were almost certainly among those who attended the inauguration of the magnificent twin-spired church at Sechelt (p. 34). A contemporary newspaper report describes the arrangements made. *Since last November preparations have been going on for the opening of the [Sechelt] church, and at all the missions the Indians have been saving their money to be present on the occasion. The C.P.R. had granted very low rates [to] those coming from interior points and furnished a special train, which arrived in Vancouver yesterday morning, bringing in about 400. Others had come down by the regular trains of Sunday, Monday and Tuesday, so that the delegation from the inland numbered nearly 1,000 souls. Those from the north coast came down in goodly numbers by canoes. The tribes represented in yesterday's gathering were from Thlayamin, Sechelt, Squamish, Stalo, Douglas Lake, Lillooet, Shuswap, Thompson River, Williams Lake, Douglas Lake, Chilcotin, Stewart's Lake, Stickeen and Yookooptah. They were all accompanied by their respective*

missionaries, namely, *Rev. Fathers Chirouse, jr., Corneillier, Peythevin, Le Jeune, Chirouse, sr., Le Jacque* [Jacq], *Marechal* [Marchal] *and Maurice* [Morice] (*Daily World*, 4 June 1890).

Although the spire at Bonaparte is a simplified version of those at Sechelt, it appears incongruously elaborate because the rest of the building has so little decoration. What decorative details there are, however, are as well finished as the spire, and repetition of the simple rounded arches in the windows and the main door contributes a sense of unity and order. As it was in the early 1900s, before the sacristy and living quarters were added, the tall white church stood in vivid contrast to the low rough buildings of the village (p. 134).

Handmade locally, the unusually wide door is recessed in the main entrance arch; it is not board-and-batten but is, rather, an excellent example of false paneling, its strips of molding arranged in the conventional pattern. In place of the usual glazed transom above, the builder has used tongue-and-groove boards with a beaded edge and then cut them with a series of arched openings.

On the end wall of the interior and following the full curve of the barrel vaulted ceiling is a nimbus created by alternating segments of tongue-and-groove boards focusing on the sacred heart. Below it, the richly decorated altar is probably an import from Montreal.

Simple, locally made pews stand against the dado, or wainscot, which is built of tongue-and-groove boards with their edges beaded. At waist height, the dado gives way to a board-and-batten wall covering.

Cariboo-Chilcotin

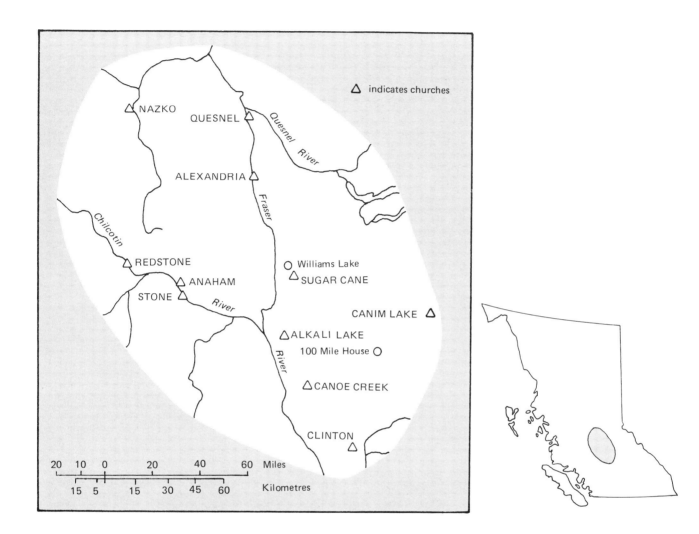

In the Cariboo and Chilcotin districts, deeply eroded valleys drain an undulating plateau where elevations range between 900 and 1200 metres (3000 and 4000 feet). The area's principal rivers are the Fraser, running south from Quesnel to Lillooet, and the Chilcotin and Chilko, flowing to the Fraser past Alexis Creek.

Coastal mountains shelter the region from heavy rainfall — annual precipitation averages only 38 – 50 cm. (15″ – 20″). On the plateau winters are cold, with three to five months below freezing point, and mean summer temperatures range between 12 and 16° C (55 – 60° F). The valleys are slightly warmer in both summer and winter.

Sparse forests of coniferous and deciduous trees dot the area. Wide benches of grassland, which settlers were to find a natural rangeland for cattle, flank the rivers. Caribou, elk, deer, moose, rabbit, and waterfowl are all plentiful in this region.

The Lillooet people of the Interior Salish group live in the south of the Cariboo. Three subgroups of the Athapaskan language group also inhabit the area: the Chilcotin, who live in the Chilcotin River basin; the Shuswap, who live near the Fraser River at Clinton, Canoe Creek, Alkali Lake, Sugar Cane, and Canim Lake; and the Carrier, who live at Quesnel, Alexandria, and Nazko. Trade with coastal groups led to some alteration in their social structures, but the material culture of all these groups remained substantially that of Interior bands. All the Cariboo-Chilcotin tribes lived in small, nomadic family groupings for most of the year and sustained themselves by hunting, gathering, and fishing. Today, ranching provides employment for many.

Churches throughout the area lacked strongly defined regional features, though some buildings — like the church at Sugar Cane — were and still are extremely handsome and refined.

Roman Catholic Church

REDSTONE

Built c. 1910

Pointed windows in rectangular panels
and a robust looking belfry make this
church at Redstone a simpler and
rougher version of the one at Stone (p.
142). The windows used here are disproportionately deep, extending almost
to the floor, and they were very probably
salvaged from a former church with
higher walls, in keeping with the design
of many earlier buildings.

While the building looks weathered
and lacks trim on the roof and door,
there is evidence that it is both used and
cared for. A concrete foundation and a
tight roof over the old shingles make it
weatherproof, and the woodpile is
clearly for use in the iron stove so
common in early Indian churches.

Roman Catholic Church

NAZKO

n.d.

Nazko is a village to the northwest of Quesnel. Until recently, it was only accessible by horse or on foot.

The church was certainly constructed after 1915 and may date as late as 1920. By that time one of the techniques used in its construction had been abandoned for some years in most areas of the province. In the front portion of the building, the vertical studs of the wall have been set in notches cut for them in the sills at ground level — a transitional technique, characteristic of the phase when post-and-beam began to give way to balloon-frame construction.

In the same part of the church, its builder has used poles instead of milled lumber for the rafters, a practice typical of rough rural building. The rear section, which is unquestionably a later addition, has milled lumber for its rafters and does not have notched sill beams.

Treatment of the window opening also varies between the two sections. The front portion has windows treated like those at Anaham (p. 141) and Stone (p. 142). In the rear portion, a slightly more pointed sash is set in the wall without trim.

Church of the Sacred Heart of Jesus

ROMAN CATHOLIC

ANAHAM

Dedicated 1923

Between 1870 and 1871, before he was ordained, Brother George Blanchet directed the building of a log church at Anaham, a large village in a broad valley near Alexis Creek. Even by 1900, however, there was apparently a need for a new and larger building, and the present church was built by a Tommy Meldrum in the early 1920s.

Although the combination of pointed arch and rectangular trim in the windows and the proportions of the belfry are like those of the church at Stone (p. 142), the appeal of these features has been lost in this later and larger building. The belfry, particularly, has lost character; the designer has omitted gables on its roof and given the openings a dull rectangular shape rather than the attractive arched form seen at Stone.

Structurally, the building has not lasted well. Vertical log buttresses are now set into the ground on each side in front of the first and third windows. Cables through the interior connect the tops of these buttresses which prevent the walls from collapsing under the weight of the roof. Inside, one of the cables is stretched taut about six feet above the altar rails, which have been retained in this church despite liturgical changes.

The altar itself also remains intact. According to Father François Thomas, a longtime pioneer missionary of the region, it was made by two young carpenters from Alkali Lake. Such help from neighbouring villages was extremely common. Modern materials now dominate the interior; plywood and pressed paperboard cover the walls, and the ceiling has been tiled.

Church of St. John the Baptist

ROMAN CATHOLIC

STONE

Built 1904

As the churches at Sugar Cane, Canim Lake, and Canoe Creek have similar design features, so do the churches at Stone, Anaham (p. 141), and Redstone (p. 139). Of the latter three, the building at Stone is the most successful.

In the Cariboo-Chilcotin, buildings continued to be constructed of logs for longer and in greater numbers than elsewhere. Even today it is not an unusual building method in this region. The thickness of the walls at Stone (about 25 cm.) implies hewn log construction, but clapboard has been used to make the church imitate a frame building and give it a more stylish and up-to-date appearance. Whether the disguise was added some years after initial construction to give the church a facelift, or whether it was always covered, is not clear. Aluminum sheets like those on the roof here frequently mask the original shingles of old interior churches. Several panels have blown off to reveal the earlier roofing.

Set into the clapboard-covered walls and facade, the windows have an odd combination of rectangular trim and arched sashes. This pattern is unique to the Chilcotin area and found at both Anaham and Redstone.

Inside, a lozenge frieze similar to the one at St. Paul's, Alexandria (p. 146) can be seen clearly at the rear but has

been removed at the front. At one time
it ran completely round the interior.
The altar rail and gates are also of the
same design as those at St. Paul's, and
the two altars have the same kind of
chamfered columns. The design of this
one, however, is much simpler.

St. Peter's Church

ROMAN CATHOLIC

QUESNEL

Built 1904-10

Close to Quesnel is an area referred to as Red Bluff, named after the red stone of the nearby wooded cliffs above the Fraser. In 1904 an Indian band settled on a flat in the Red Bluff area, named their settlement Egypt after Jacob the Patriarch's land of plenty, and began work on a log church. They added cove siding to the building in 1910.

Although plain, the exterior is given a little relief by the octagonal roof on the tower and a round window above the sanctuary. Vandals have broken up the interior furnishings for firewood, but part of the robustly turned altar rail remains; so does the altar, although its

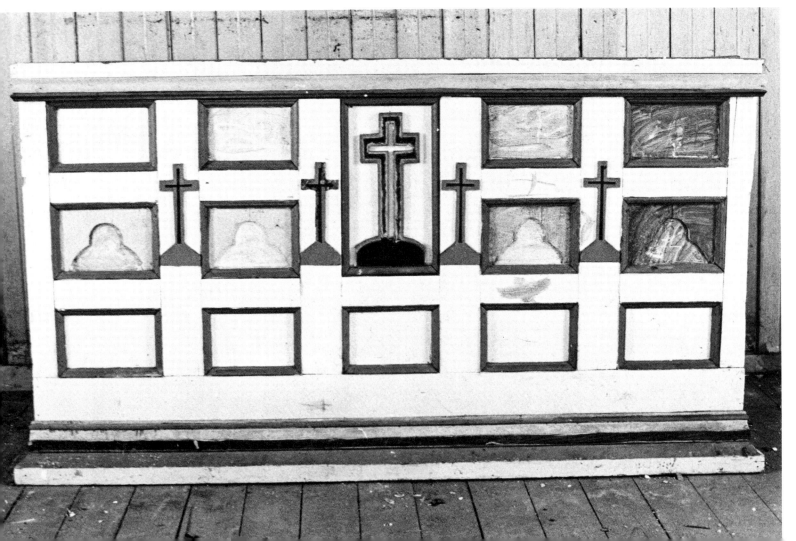

decoration of applied crosses and central row of panels is defaced. The badly applied paint in the panels is watercolour and not original. The outline of the complete original altar is just visible on the wall.

St. Paul's Church

ROMAN CATHOLIC

ALEXANDRIA

Built 1906

At Alexandria the Fraser River has several benches on each side. St. Paul's stands on one of these near the east bank and is the third church in a village where Father Modeste Demers first said mass in 1842. As most of the community has moved to the west of the river, and there is no bridge, the building is only used for such ceremonies as weddings and funerals.

St. Paul's dates from 1906, according to Father Thomas's memoirs, and was built by a Willy Shepherd. Although the horizontal divisions of his belfry are too numerous and dominant to create a unified composition, it is a very striking and inventive construction. Its effects were achieved by building a series of simple boxes and decorating their surfaces with strips and triangles of wood. Unfortunately, the more recent aluminum roof tends to isolate the belfry from the main portion of the building, and the lack of paint on the belfry itself contributes to this impression.

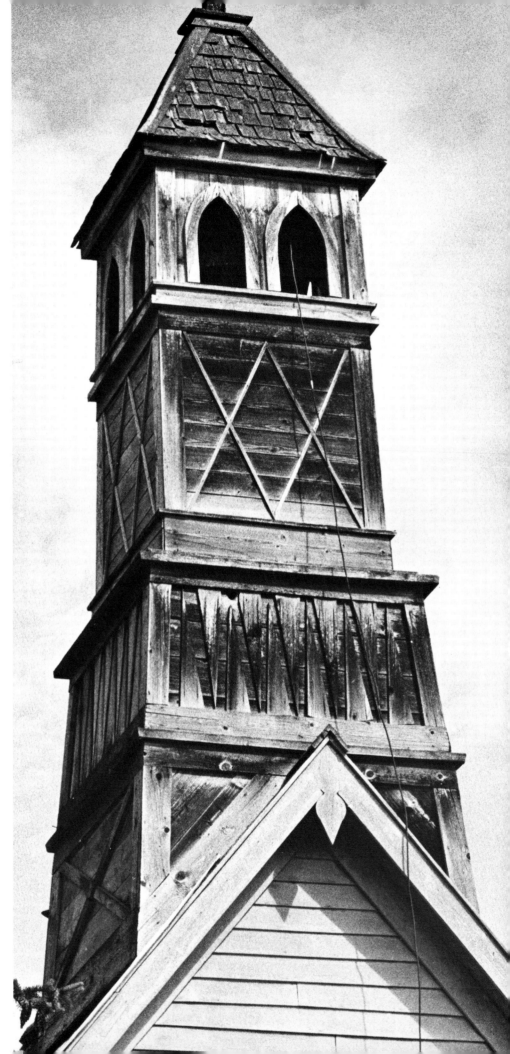

Despite the church's infrequent use, all the interior furnishings remain, including the simple chamfered altar rails. White walls and a powder blue ceiling decorated at the cornice by an unusual lozenge and dentil frieze form a light and airy setting for the hand-made altar. Flanked by two wall shrines with frames cut in the sawtooth pattern common in all folk art, this altar was probably constructed locally. Its style and manner of construction using a series of overlapping boards to imitate paneling are similar to those of the belfry.

147

Roman Catholic Church

CANOE CREEK

Built 1900

Two years were required to raise the funds necessary to build this church at Canoe Creek, midway between 70 Mile House and Clinton. In order to help their Canoe Creek neighbours replace the older, log church constructed in the late 1860s, the people of Canim Lake permitted them to trap in Canim Lake territory. The balance of the building money came from the Canoe Creek band's cattle-ranching activities.

According to Father Thomas's records, the contract to build the church was let for $1,200 to a Mr. Jimmy Brown, a skilled, part Indian carpenter who had apparently studied at the Oblate college in New Westminster. He finished construction in time for the church to open in October 1900, when a lamp brought from Quebec was hung above and in front of the altar in the sanctuary.

Some of the design features of the churches at both Sugar Cane (p. 153) and Bonaparte (p. 134) influenced Brown's exterior decoration, although his work is less complex. The stepped door trim of overlapping boards imitates the more elegant arched trim at Sugar Cane; the sawtooth fretwork of the eaves and the fan and sawtooth trim of the gable window are similar to the cemetery-gate decoration at Bonaparte. This fret decoration on the eaves, incidentally, extends even to the back gable; such trim is normally confined to the facade.

Generally, little effort was made to improve the landscape around the small rural churches of the province's dry Interior. But mature lilac bushes soften the lines of the exterior at Canoe Creek. They are found also at Alkali Lake and Canim Lake.

148

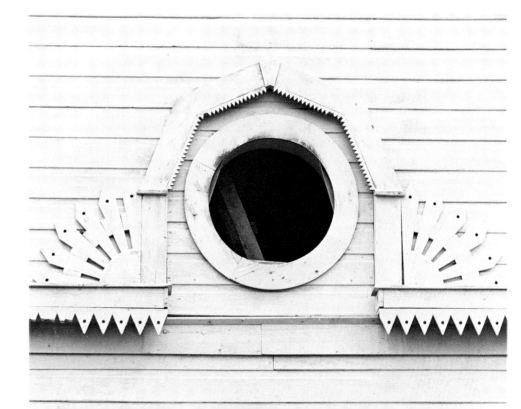

Even more than the exterior, the altar at Canoe Creek, with its pedestaled arched reredos, owes a debt to the church at Sugar Cane. Its identical rope-design spindles are from the same supplier, but they are arranged differently. Because the interior is so simple — the pews particularly so — the altar becomes a more forceful focal point than in some more elaborate buildings. The regular dark marks running along the front of the sanctuary indicate where the balusters of the altar rail were originally fastened.

Church of St. Theresa of the Child Jesus

ROMAN CATHOLIC

ALKALI LAKE

Built 1890, enlarged 1921-22

The first sight after climbing the short, steep hill up to the village of Alkali Lake is Father Thomas's old, life-size crucifix. The building to which it is fastened is the result partly of work done in 1890 and partly of extensive renovations undertaken in the 1920s.

Alkali Lake's original log church was built in 1866. The second, with a two-bayed nave, attached sanctuary, and tower centred in the facade, replaced it in 1890. When the need arose to enlarge this church, the rebuilders destroyed the sanctuary, added transepts and extended the nave.

Asphalt shingle siding designed to imitate shakes does not enhance this pleasantly proportioned building. The exterior otherwise lacks outstanding features, but it is interesting to see, on either side of the arched entrance, the altar rails now acting as a kind of porch railing. And the foundations, which are typical of Interior churches, have hardly been concealed at all. They consist of large natural boulders set at intervals along the main beams and at the corners.

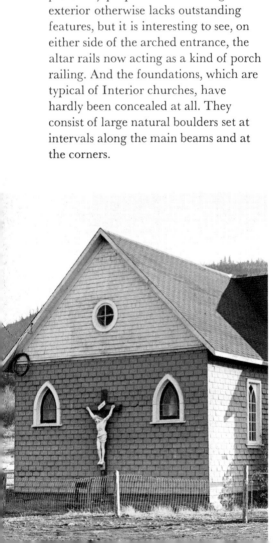

Inside the church, in spite of the few windows for the size of the building, pale colours create the illusion of a light-filled space. Oddly, only the upper halves of double-hung sashes are used for the windows on either side of the altar.

The main altar appears higher and narrower than it originally did; the platform which supported the altar and gave it a broad base has been removed, and as a result there is a gap between the altar top and the reredos or altar screen attached to the wall behind. This gap has been disguised by tacking a cloth to the bottom of the reredos.

Some of the interior trim here is unique, such as the sawn and carved star on the ceiling at the crossing of the transepts and the notched and chamfered choir supports. Other parts, like the spindles of the choir rail, are of a type available in quantity from millwork shops.

Church of the Immaculate Conception

ROMAN CATHOLIC

SUGAR CANE

Built 1895

Father François Thomas arrived in British Columbia from France in 1894. After initial training under Bishop Durieu, he was assigned to the St. Joseph's mission at Williams Lake.

Father Thomas records that the village of Sugar Cane at the south end of Williams Lake took its name from the meadow on which the band settled in 1881. The meadow itself was so named *on account of its tall grass, which was much loved by horses.* At the opening of the village church in July 1895, Father Le Jeune was impressed enough to write that *everything is of perfect finish, both outside and inside.* And the high quality of finish is still one of the most striking characteristics of this tightly designed and well-constructed building.

In every detail, the facade is the epitome of balanced design. The delicately pointed arch motif unifies the symmetrical rectangular and triangular areas formed by the uprights of the tower corners and the horizontals running across them. Here, the bull's eye window seems to serve as a restful focus more successfully than in any of the other early churches. The simple dignity and refinement of the entrance is achieved by a succession of overlapping, progressively smaller board arches.

No interior of an Indian village church in British Columbia has more attractive and well-made board-and-batten walls than Sugar Cane. Its cornice repeats the delicate board arches of the facade where it meets the complex tongue-and-groove ceiling; its regular arcade gives the interior a strong sense of order.

A rare combination of stained and painted wood gives the altar its distinctive character. The upper, stained portion may, in fact, have been stripped and refinished. Thin plywood appears to be covering the two large columns at the side. Underneath they may be fluted and match the two smaller columns just above the tabernacle. If the building were crude, it would probably be correct to assume that the congregation had imported this altar. In this case, although the molded motif of the sacred heart is a mass-produced item, the high quality of workmanship evident in both the church and the altar suggests that the same expert craftsmen worked on both. The unusually graceful pews and the altar rail, now discarded, are equally well made.

To the rear of the interior, the choir and its supporting piers frame the entry in a carefully studied composition. Excellent design also shows in the way the builder has organized the stairway to the choir; in many rural churches, they are situated very awkwardly.

155

St. Peter's Church

ROMAN CATHOLIC

CLINTON

Built 1892

In 1864, Bishop Louis D'Herbomez became the first bishop of the mainland of British Columbia. It was during his period of office that the majority of Roman Catholic missions to the Indians were established.

By 1869 he had blessed the first church in Clinton village, a settlement close to the ten-year-old Cariboo wagon road which led north to the goldfields. Thirty-three years later, in 1892, the Pavilion villagers and other volunteers helped Father Maurice Marchal to replace the old church.

Like its predecessor, the new building was of log, and it probably incorporated some materials salvaged from the earlier structure. Its plan was a common one — a two-bayed nave with attached sanctuary and a dominant entrance tower centred in the facade — but it was among the most primitive of all the British Columbia Indian churches recorded in photographs. As at Seton Portage (p. 125), only the facade was covered in siding; but the exposed log structure here appeared far rougher. The shortness of the tower gave the building a brooding quality.

Although Father Thomas once claimed that Father Marchal was an excellent carpenter, the appearance of the Clinton church provided no evidence to justify such a reputation.

In 1951, this church was torn down, and a new frame building, also named St. Peter's, took its place.

156

St. Augustine's Church

ROMAN CATHOLIC

CANIM LAKE

Built 1897

St. Augustine's elaborate entrance of overlapping board arches immediately recalls the doorway of the church at Sugar Cane (p. 153), built two years earlier. Despite the slightly inappropriate use of shakes instead of shingles to repair the roof, the facade of this church is very attractive. A bull's eye window set in a measured blind arcade like the one at Sugar Cane provides a single focus, and strong horizontals at the top and bottom of the gable emphasize solidity and permanence. The notching of the three brackets above the Gothic portal is a much more naive detail and appears slightly inconsistent with the rest of the design.

Shrines like the one to the right of the entrance are not as common as they once were. Exposed to the elements, they quickly deteriorate unless they are very well cared for.

Sugar Cane's influence is as evident in the interior of the church as it is in the facade. The arcaded frieze and a cornice made of heavy built-up molding are more elaborate than those at the earlier church, and the main columns of the reredos behind the altar are of a more handsome design. The spiral reeding on the main portion of their shafts is both unusual and impressive. Two alternating spindle designs make up the altar rail, which, in this church, has survived the recent changes in the liturgy.

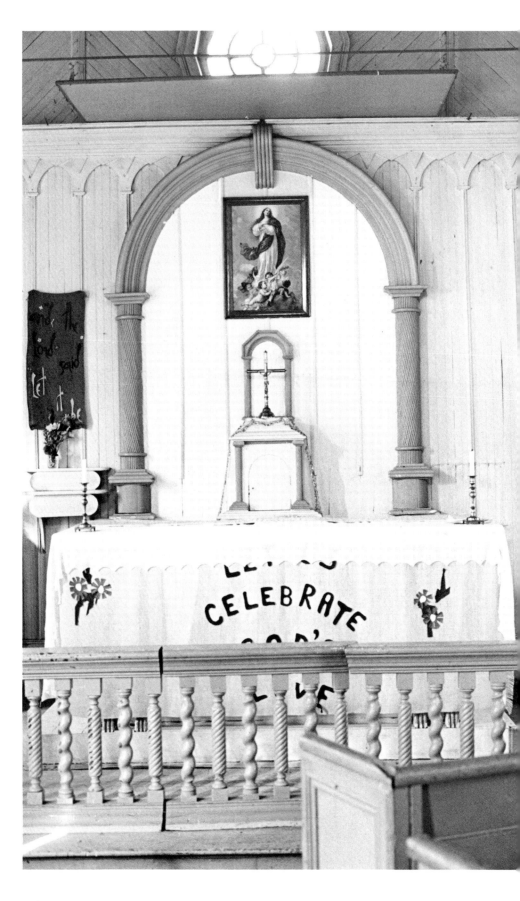

Bulkley-Nechako

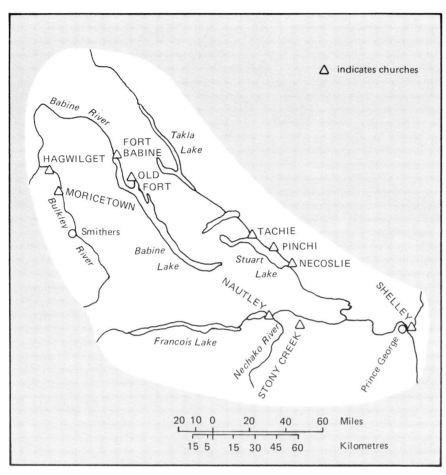

The Nechako, Stuart, and Bulkley rivers drain a mountainous region of many long and narrow lakes to the west and northwest of Prince George.

Winters in this area are generally long and cold — the January mean daily maximum is only —11° C (13° F). Summers are short and cool — the mean summer temperature is only 13–16° C (55–60° F), and the region's mean maximum is 18–21°C (65–70° F). Temperatures dip below 0° C (32° F) for between four and six months of the year. Precipitation averages 50 cm. (20″) per year, almost 40 per cent of which comes in the form of snow.

Forests in the region are largely coniferous, interspersed in the river valleys with deciduous stands. Game includes deer and caribou, and waterfowl and fish are abundant. The Carrier people, an Athapaskan language subgroup, inhabit the region. Hunting and fishing traditionally provided most of their food needs, and the various bands built semipermanent villages at fishing centres such as Moricetown and Hagwilget. The salmon runs are still of great importance in the region. Their houses were constructed of bark and plank and were similar to, although smaller than, those of the Indian groups living on the coast.

Most of the early churches in this part of the province were Roman Catholic buildings. Many were extremely impressive, but lacked regional architectural distinctiveness. Their interiors often still contain well-made furnishings and fine decoration. The board-and-batten walls at Pinchi and Tachie, for instance, are superb examples of local workmanship.

Church of St. Mary Magdalen

ROMAN CATHOLIC

HAGWILGET

Built 1908

Hagwilget marked the edge of Roman Catholic mission territory. Protestant denominations shared the area beyond Hagwilget to the coast and the north. The church is impressively situated on a hill overlooking the Hagwilget Canyon of the Bulkley River a few miles from its junction with the Skeena at Hazelton. With its many crosses and pinnacles, the church is an outstanding landmark.

Originally, the ridge of the roof had fretwork cresting like that at Necoslie (p. 173), but it has not survived. The tower itself, however, has a fine combination of decorative details. On either side of the main door the tongue-and-groove panels direct the eye upwards first to a rather fussy pointed window and then to the extraordinary bull's eye window above it. A ring of knife-and-fork-like shapes made of sawn wood, painted gold, decorates it and possibly represents a radiant host. Above this window, the pinnacles and spire continue the upward movement.

Church of Our Lady of the Rosary

ROMAN CATHOLIC

MORICETOWN

Built 1912-13

Of all the early Roman Catholic missionaries, Father Adrien G. Morice is probably the most widely remembered. An anthropologist and historian as well as a priest, he wrote many pioneer volumes on the Indians and history of northern British Columbia. Moricetown is named for him. The present church was built some years after he had left the area. It shows the same decidedly professional work as Nautley (p. 172), although the design of this building, with its dominant tower, bellcast roof, and generally strong vertical thrust is far more impressive. The apsidal sanctuary, particularly, is an unusual refinement; the only other example nearby is at the much earlier St. Paul's, Kitwanga (p. 69). In spite of the high standards of building evident in this church, however, the facade seems to have been designed independently of the interior; the large main windows are cut in half by the floor of the choir gallery.

A handsome building, Our Lady of the Rosary nevertheless lacks some of the interest given by the fanciful workmanship nearly always found throughout earlier buildings. The interior, finished in painted pressed paperboard, is light and spacious, but it is dull, and

such details as the altar rails have a
heavy appearance. The robust turned
balusters of these rails are of a type
made in quantity locally for use in
cemetery fences. The altar itself is very
ponderous and depends almost entirely
on commercial plaster reliefs and
figures for decorative effect.

Roman Catholic Church

FORT BABINE

Built 1915

Early in the last century, the Hudson's Bay Company established Fort Babine on Babine Lake as a post on the route between Fort St. James and the coast, but no company post exists there now. An early church in the village had a spire similar to the soaring one at Necoslie (p. 173). Although the Fort Babine spire was less lofty, it was more boldly decorated; and when this old church was torn down after completion of the new building in 1915, the spire was retained as an entrance to the churchyard. It still stood there in 1926 (opp. page, top), but unfortunately it no longer exists.

The entire exterior of the 1915 church (this page), except for the stately, Georgian-inspired window trim and the doors, is covered in embossed sheet iron made to resemble rough-cut masonry. Its spire came in kit form, like the ones at Shelley (p. 180), to be mounted on the wooden frame. With the coming of the railway, Burns Lake to the south became the supply point for the Babine Lake area; the embossed sheet iron, together with other materials and some of the furnishings for the Fort Babine church, was therefore shipped there from the east by rail and hauled across the ice to Fort Babine in the winter. At least one of the sheets of siding still shows the shipping stencil reading *Father Coccola, Burns Lake, B.C.* Although the building is of wooden balloon-frame construction, its simple design is in keeping with the imitation stone wall covering.

Only a naive symbolic painting of the Lamb, possibly made locally, on the dull imported altar is of note in the interior of this building, which has been walled with modern plywood paneling.

Roman Catholic Church

OLD FORT

Built 1925

Although the design of the church spire at Old Fort is based upon that of the imported iron one at Fort Babine (p. 164), it is of more interest because of its added decorative details, such as the elaborate cornices above and below the drum, its square corner pinnacles, and the pediments ornamented with stylized lilies. The triple-arched entrance in the tower below is unfinished and somewhat ill conceived (the centre arch, for example, breaks the cornice very awk-

wardly), but it has a paradoxical appeal. Completely unconventional features of the design are the two side doors, which provide direct access to the choir, while the centre door leads, as is usual, to the nave. In contrast to the frame construction of the entrance and tower, the main walls are hewn logs covered with shingles.

Interest inside the building lies primarily in a number of details such as the cut, carved, and painted decoration of the tabernacle and the freehand drilled brackets of the choir supports. An end view of an ordinary cornice exposed in the choir gallery is also interesting because it illustrates how the large complex moldings found in a great many of these early wooden churches were built up of smaller strips.

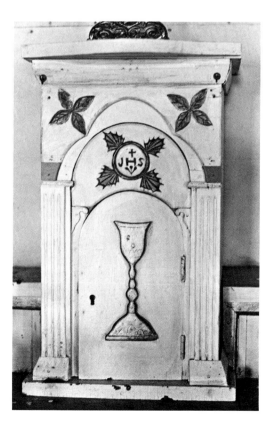

Church of St. Cecilia

ROMAN CATHOLIC

TACHIE

Built 1872, rebuilt 1913

Repeated flooding, as at nearby Pinchi (p. 170), forced the Tachie villagers in 1913 to dismantle, move, and rebuild their log-walled church on higher ground, where it now overlooks Stuart Lake. Apart from the homemade plywood doors, the exterior looks much as it did following the 1913 reconstruction.

Bold red corner capping and horizontals trim the stark and startling pure white facade. The bell mounted in the frame tower dates from 1872, when the church was originally built. It came from France by steamship and riverboat and completed its journey to Tachie by dugout canoe from Fort St. James.

Much of the interior, particularly the sanctuary, has been extensively re-sheathed in modern materials: mahogany plywood paneling on the walls and slab doors, for example. But most of the original board-and-batten nave wall is intact, and it is very similar to the one at Pinchi.

Admirably complementing the fine wall at Tachie are two exuberantly curved brackets designed to support statuettes. Sawn locally, they blend with this environment much better than would the more frequently found mass-produced examples made of plaster.

Board-and-batten is, after the more easily installed tongue-and-groove, the most popular early wall finish in British Columbian rural churches. It has a stronger texture than tongue-and-groove and is usually completed with either an angular sawtooth frieze like the one at Pinchi or a frieze cut to form an arcade.

Construction of a board-and-batten wall begins by covering the top ends of the vertical boards with a wider horizontal board. This board has been previously cut into arches spaced according to the width of the vertical boards — in this case, about ten inches. When this stage is completed, narrower molded battens are nailed over the joints between the vertical boards. Sometimes small capitals, made of short lengths of molding with the cut ends suitably carved, further enrich the effect. The top edge of the arcaded board frieze is finished by a heavy cornice built of a series of molded strips.

Holy Cross Church

ROMAN CATHOLIC

PINCHI

Built 1871, moved 1930-40

A small exposed-log building with a
simple exterior, Holy Cross is one of the
oldest churches remaining in northern
British Columbia.

Pinchi is located on Pinchi Creek
where it enters Stuart Lake, and,
because of repeated flooding, the villagers decided in the 1930s to move this
building a short distance up a rise to
higher ground, where it continued in
use until the early 1960s. The church is
now being refurbished, and the bell and
its timber frame, now resting to the
right of the door, will be returned to
where they were once mounted on the
roof.

Reached through a weatherbeaten
handmade door with a low-relief
carving of the sacred heart on a cross
fixed to its central member, the colour-
ful interior is quite unexpected. The
boards of the wall are painted soft green
and the battens over the joints, soft
blue. Burnt sienna moldings trim the
ivory-painted sawtooth frieze.

Besides one or two statues, only two
items of furniture remain: an unusually
light and graceful altar rail of fret
balusters is identical to that at Necoslie
(p. 173), and the altar, with its
imported plaster reliefs is well
proportioned in relation to its
setting in a small sanctuary.

St. Peter's Church

ROMAN CATHOLIC

NAUTLEY

Built c. 1914

The building of the railway early in this century brought a large influx of settlers to the Bulkley and Nechako valleys. Among the settlers were professional carpenters and builders who probably played a great part in building this church at Nautley, near Fort Fraser. Its only unusual details are found in the facade. The walls of the lower tower slope inwards, giving the facade a slightly uncomfortable appearance, and it is odd to find a circular louvred opening in the spire roof rather than in the tower proper; leaks seem to be invited. Inside, the church has been modernized.

Brick chimneys and a concrete foundation, neatly applied siding, and windows conventionally scaled and placed may seem luxurious features when a church like St. Peter's is compared with some of the other rural churches, but they are simply typical of any well-constructed, less isolated building.

Church of Our Lady of Good Hope

ROMAN CATHOLIC

NECOSLIE

Built 1873-74

A temporary church named St. Paul's was built at Necoslie, near Fort St. James, in 1869, probably by Father Jean-Marie Le Jacq on his first visit. Work on a larger church began in 1873, when Fathers Le Jacq and Blanchet arrived to make the mission a permanent establishment.

While Stuart Lake was still frozen in the spring, the villagers pulled the logs for the new church about three miles across the ice to the building site on the opposite shore. According to Louis Billy Prince of Fort St. James, who was seven at the time, it took a day to transport two logs by this method. Once the basic log structure was complete, the building was given a buttressed tower and a low roof (top).

After 1905, when Father Coccola took over the mission, the building was remodeled to look much as it does today (bottom). The tower was extended, the spire was built, and siding was put over the log walls. Arched windows replaced rectangular ones in the sanctuary, but not elsewhere. A local craftsman named Benoit Prince carved a large globe and chamfered cross for the top of the spire. Prominent cresting decorated the ridge of the roof at this time, and it even continued down the edges of the gables. All this cresting has now disappeared, but, fortunately, the spire trim remains intact.

One of the most impressive in the province, the spire is decorated with a large number of exaggeratedly pointed details: pointed arched openings in the drum, with a row of gables above; pinnacles at each corner; and an openwork lozenge frieze. All of the shingles are scalloped, whereas the more usual pattern was for bands of plain and cut shingles to alternate.

The spire is such a triumph that other fine but much less spectacular details of the exterior are apt to be overlooked. These include the graceful ogee arch of the door in the front of the tower and the main entrance door in the side of the tower surmounted by a sawn cross.

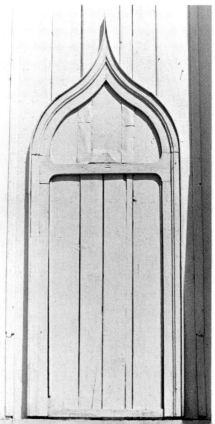

174

Minor interior details such as the fret brackets on the choir supports and the scrolled legs of the coffin stands are equally interesting.

Sheet iron embossed with fleurs-de-lis now sheathes the whole of the interior. It was added during the 1905 remodeling and very closely resembles the iron used to cover the interior at St. Mary's, Deadman Creek (p. 106). At the same time, a very plain choir gallery was built to create extra seating room.

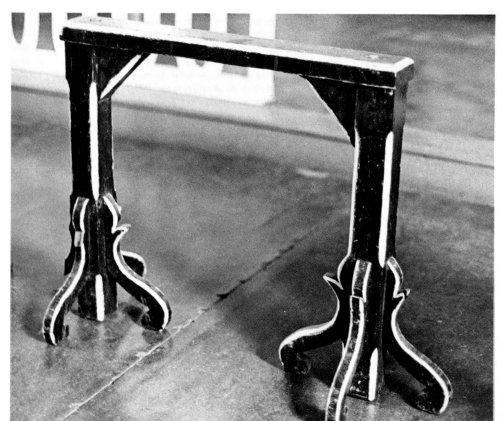

176

Despite the remodeling, some early features remain, notably the excellent four-panel doors on each side of the altar and the altar rails, which are identical to those at Pinchi (p. 170). The doors were handmade and decorated with applied moldings. Throughout the interior the moldings are now painted bright red or green, and the windows, although ordinary sashes, are glazed with alternate panes of clear and ruby red glass. As a result, strong colours punctuate the plain interior.

Roman Catholic Church

STONY CREEK

Dedicated 1924

The old well-built log churches could be extremely strong. When the congregation at Stony Creek, a village about fifteen miles southwest of Vanderhoof, set about tearing their old church down to build this new one in the early 1920s, they needed a team of horses to pull the walls apart.

The new building was constructed on a rise above the rocky creekbed from which the village takes its name. The church is plain but well proportioned, although its appearance has been spoiled by the plywood boards in the triple-arched tower window. Also unfortunate aesthetically is the contrast between the corrugated iron which now sheathes the spire and the expert shingling on the roof proper.

Plaster was rarely used in early rural churches because at the time they were built it was not readily available outside cities. However, it could be obtained for use at Stony Creek because the railway linked Vanderhoof with the larger population centres even before the 1920s. The uniform finish that the plaster gives to the interior walls and arched sanctuary moldings contrasts well with the neatly installed and richly

178

stained woodwork. And it is the plaster, of course, which makes the smooth curve of the sanctuary itself possible, a curve not reflected in the exterior of the building.

Repeating in its design the triple arches of the tower window and the sanctuary, the altar is simple and pleasant but not outstanding. Its steps have been removed, leaving a dark unpainted and unadorned plinth.

Imported mass-produced materials frequently served as the models for local handmade imitations and variations. The pews at Stony Creek are an example. Factory-made, they were clearly the inspiration for the handmade ones at Fountain (p. 130).

179

Church of St. Pius X

ROMAN CATHOLIC

SHELLEY

Built 1913

In 1911, after two years of negotiations, the Grand Trunk Pacific Railway (later part of the CNR) purchased the reserve at Fort George as the townsite for what is now Prince George. The Indian people from the reserve were resettled on the Fraser a few miles to the east. Here, the new village of Shelley and this impressive church were built.

Overlooking the main means of transportation, the river, the church's striking facade owes little to local artistry. Its distinctive decorative features — as opposed to its main structure, which is of wood — are all of embossed sheet iron fitted over the basic wooden frame of the building itself. Even the roofing, some of which can be seen below the arched openings near the top of the tower, is of iron embossed to look like shingles. Architectural components of this kind, such as the complete curvilinear spires and the arches supporting them, came from Quebec factories in kit form. Individual elements were then nailed to a framework constructed on site. Few churches in British Columbia incorporate such materials, though they were commonly used in commercial storefronts of the period. Their use must have involved considerable expense. Funding for the sheet iron and for such elaborate details of the church as the stained glass in the windows probably came from the settlement with the railway company.

One of the few remaining examples of local workmanship inside the church is a single old pew of the park bench type. Apart from this well-made piece and the colour given by the exceptional windows, each depicting a different saint,

the interior of the church is plain and unappealing. Although the windows are unsigned, the ponderous tabernacle bears the label of *Crevier & Fils. Dessinateurs et Fabricants Emeublements Eglise Menuiserie d'Art etc., Montréal.* They may also have supplied the windows. Quebec was the source for many of the elaborate and factory-made church furnishings in early British Columbia Roman Catholic churches.

In most rural Roman Catholic churches the tabernacle remains, despite liturgical developments, in the centre at the back of the altar. Here, however, it has been moved to the pedestal that probably first supported the statue that now stands to the right on a small table. This rearrangement enables the priest to celebrate mass from behind the altar and to face his congregation without the tabernacle standing in the way.

181

Preservation and Restoration

JOHN VEILLETTE, GARY WHITE

During the course of our photographic fieldwork, the rich historical heritage embodied in British Columbia's early churches became increasingly apparent. At the same time, the problems of preserving both the character and fabric of these buildings impressed themselves upon us with greater and greater force. A photographic record is important, but it is no substitute for the actual churches. In conversation from time to time we discussed the possibility of working on one of the churches after completing our fieldwork. As it turned out, we were to work on two of the most interesting buildings still standing in the Skeena-Nass area, St. Paul's at Kitwanga and the Salvation Army Citadel at Glen Vowell.

ST. PAUL'S, KITWANGA

When in the fall of 1973 our fieldwork came to an end, we were at Hazelton, and the Reverend Robert Warren invited us to carry out preservation and restoration work on the churches under his care. Of these, St. Paul's, Kitwanga, built in the early 1890s, was one of the most impressive and historically valuable early Indian churches in the province. There was no question in our minds that it should be preserved if possible.

Although we started work as volunteers, funding for the undertaking eventually came from a variety of sources. A federal government Local Initiative Project (LIP) grant provided wages; and the provincial government's First Citizen's Fund, the diocese, and the parish assisted by paying for certain capital expenses.

The ideal location for our restoration headquarters at Kitwanga was the vicarage of St. Paul's. Originally the home of the manager of the Kitwanga Hudson's Bay store, it was built of hewn logs in the 1920s and later converted for use by Kitwanga's resident clergyman. However, by 1973 no priest had lived in Kitwanga on a permanent basis for several years, and the building had deteriorated badly. Before work on St. Paul's could begin, we had to repair the vicarage.

Lack of suitable headquarters was not our only barrier to making a start on the church. From the first, it was difficult to find people who would work for the wages permitted under the LIP system. But eventually, with a crew composed initially of women from the village, we cleaned and repainted the vicarage and then began to determine what work the church itself needed.

Since the winters are fairly severe in this region of the province, we postponed the exterior work and started inside the church. The interior walls were in good condition. Only a few water stains near the cornices marred the original dark brown varnish. We covered these marks with a stain and varnish that matched the original finish and continued by repainting the floor and the window and door trim a reddish-brown colour. The sashes

Refinishing prayer-desk at Kitwanga

Deteriorating tower roof, Kitwanga

themselves were removed, given minor repairs, and then reglazed where necessary before we repainted them in their original colour — white.

Most of the church furniture required little more treatment than a thorough cleaning and waxing. The varnish on the prayer desk, however, had become very badly cracked and flaked, and the organ, too, needed stripping and refinishing. In cases like these, it is best not to sand the stripped wood before refinishing in order to retain the old colour and patina of the wood. Our crew had great misgivings about stripping the organ, but when the job was completed, using a commercial paint remover and fresh varnish, they were amazed to find the instrument still had its fine (and aged) appearance.

Because the original butt hinges had failed to support the large arched cedar doors, we replaced them with larger flush-mounting hinges specially manufactured to a Gothic design. Unless there was a problem of this magnitude, however, changes to fittings were kept to a minimum in order to preserve the building's authenticity.

Having repaired the interior of the church, we turned to the exterior. Unfortunately, however, limitations on our funds for materials severely curtailed our work on this part of the building. We could not even begin to provide the two main preservation requirements: a new roof of cedar shingles and a concrete foundation.

Like many rural churches of its day, St. Paul's had a foundation that consisted solely of cedar posts sunk into the ground. This type of foundation has serious disadvantages. First, the posts are prone to rot, which eventually leads to rot in the main structural beams. The second problem occurs where the ground is wet and the weight of the building causes the foundation to settle, often unevenly. The posts had already been replaced at Kitwanga at least once because of rot, and although they were still sound, when we examined them, they were settling badly. About this problem we could do little or nothing without undertaking a large-scale operation of the type we subsequently carried out at Glen Vowell. Early buildings like St. Paul's cannot withstand uneven settling because the cut nails used in their construction are wedge shaped and, once loosened by movement, have no holding power. At Kitwanga in 1974, the siding had already begun to buckle on one side of the church for this very reason, so, before repainting, all the boards were renailed with modern wire nails, which hold better than cut ones. Giving the buildings a complete new coat of paint was our main contribution to preserving the exterior; before the paint was put on, we prepared the weathered wood thoroughly by scraping and brushing to remove any loose paint on the surface. On the roof we were only able to repair and reshingle the decorative sections below the arched louvred tower openings.

Many of the churches in the Skeena and Nass valleys have their bells housed in towers separate from the church buildings themselves. St. Paul's had one of these towers, but it was very rudimentary and in poor condition, and since it had little if any historical value, a new, more elaborate one was designed. The new tower was built of rough spruce boards on a framework of cedar poles, and, when complete, it was stained in subdued earth tones so that it would not draw attention away from the pristine white of the church. The tower blessing in the spring of 1974, when nearly all the other preservation work had been done, was the climax of the whole project.

Guests came from all the surrounding communities, and some chiefs paid up to $100 for the honour of ringing the bell. Almost $2,000 in donations were raised in this way. After the opening ceremony, the women of the village prepared and served a banquet in the community hall.

By early June 1973 when the project funding was exhausted, most of the painting was complete. Before leaving, however, we spent almost two more months in the village in order to add finishing touches.

Throughout the project, it was evident that our presence in the village was not universally welcomed. Like any small, long-established community, Kitwanga had several factions or groups with different sets of attitudes and values. Apart from occasional confrontations, these factions coexisted peacefully until an influence from outside the village shifted the balance of power in favour of one or another of them. Our project lent strength to a church-supporting faction in opposition to the band council, the elected, official authority in the village. The situation was frequently uncomfortable and occasionally explosive. Tension and opposition, however, seemed to build up the project supporters' determination to make the preservation operation a success.

SALVATION ARMY HALL, GLEN VOWELL

Our project at Glen Vowell began as a direct result of our work at Kitwanga. Glen Vowell's band manager, Alice Jeffrey, engaged us on the strength of what she had seen at St. Paul's. But while our work on St. Paul's had been a form of maintenance, the project at Glen Vowell was much larger. At this time in 1974, only the eight-hundred-square-foot shell of the village's turn-of-the-century Salvation Army hall remained. Our task had two main aspects — expansion and reconstruction. We were to direct the addition of transepts and an extension of the stage, which would increase the building's floor area by one thousand square feet. Because of the demand for these additions, it was impossible to carry out a pure exercise in restoration, but very early in the project it was agreed that these additions would conform to the style and spirit of the original building. The other major part of our task involved reconstruction of the hall's unique and distinctive triple towers shown in old photographs of the exterior.

Funds came from much the same sources that had aided the Kitwanga project, except that more volunteers were available in Glen Vowell, and the summer student employment program was placed at our disposal. Funds were also raised locally through regular community suppers, bake sales, and rummage sales. Donations supplemented these funds, and Salvation Army headquarters matched the locally raised monies with generous support grants. From the beginning, because the funding programs encouraged labour-intensive operations, we decided to use manual methods whenever possible instead of hiring modern machines.

January 1975, the first month of the project, was spent in planning and budgeting, while our crew began cutting and painting the hundreds of cedar shingles for the tower roofs. Once these were ready, work on new interior furnishings such as pews occupied most of the remaining winter months. Only a few of the early pews had survived. Since they were unattractive

Painting new bell tower, Kitwanga

Glen Vowell Citadel before restoration

185

Building new pews at Glen Vowell

Triple towers under construction, Glen Vowell

and uncomfortable, we designed and built new ones that were nevertheless appropriate to the building's age and appearance.

In the spring, while a new concrete foundation with a full basement was being prepared by a local contractor, the church interior was gutted and braced, ready for moving. Long braces were nailed to the studs near the ceiling and to the floor near the centre of the building. Braces were also nailed diagonally across the inside walls. When the new foundation was ready, we raised the building with simple hydraulic jacks, and then lowered it onto a pair of large supporting logs. These were then fastened to the floor joists. With the assistance of a team of horses and a heavy-duty "come-along" device, we dragged the entire building along greased logs onto the front portion of the new foundation.

When the building was secure, reconstruction of the triple towers began. This was the most interesting restoration problem at Glen Vowell. Using two old photographs, we determined the height of the towers by simply counting the number of pieces of siding on each one and multiplying by the width of the siding still on the remaining portion of the building. The width of the towers was evident from the building's corner framing, which was exposed when the interior was gutted; four-by-four studs had been used (instead of two-by-fours) at the points where the tower framing joined the building. Reconstruction of the unusual lattice windows was based on the form of similar decorative windows found in a few surviving gravehouses of the area. These, like the shingles, were completed in winter and stored until required in spring. The pitch of the roofs was determined by making a full-size drawing. What looks proper when laid flat on the ground, however, is not always right *in situ* — the roofs as they stand are the second attempt. The first set of rafters erected on the centre tower proved not steep enough, so a second set was designed and cut. When finally shingled even these seemed not as steeply pitched as they should have been, but the result is fairly close to the original. While this work was in progress, the end wall was removed and a local carpenter began to prepare the frames for the additional transepts and platform (chancel) area. By mid-July this framing was completed, and the summer-student-employment-program employees joined the crew.

Work resumed inside the building. Originally, plain horizontal tongue-and-groove boards sheathed the interior wall above a cedar dado of vertical, beaded-edge, tongue-and-groove boards. Mustard and brown paint had at one time covered the dado, and the walls above them had been painted white. Subsequently the interior had been resheathed and a false ceiling installed at the same time as the towers were removed. The walls had been covered with builder's paper, foil insulation, and fir plywood, except for the front, which was covered with pressed paperboard and wallpaper. The ceiling had been covered with pressed paper tiles, and the floor overlaid with a plywood subfloor and finished with a plastic floor covering.

To restore the interior to its original condition, the walls were stripped completely down to the studding and the floor down to the original floor boards. The ceiling was bared to the rough boards of the false ceiling. Because rather short nails had been used here and some had worked loose, the ceiling was renailed. Without having new tongue-and-groove boards specially milled at considerable cost, it would have been impossible to duplicate the original interior finish, which, in any case, had little appeal for the congregation. They prefered the warmth of varnished cedar. Nearly all of the interior walls, then, were entirely resheathed in standard tongue-and-groove cedar and varnished. The walls of two small offices in the building were covered with materials salvaged from the original hall. The effect of the new interior is like that of the elegant Anglican churches in this region of the province — much warmer and more churchlike than is usual for a Salvation Army citadel.

While work progressed on the interior, the reconstructed towers were nearing completion. Siding salvaged from the demolished end wall augmented siding removed from an old house which was being remodeled. In September 1975 the finials, made from sheet aluminum, were fixed to the tops of the tower roofs. By the time of the first snowfall at the end of October the exterior was complete, except for final detail painting which was done in the following spring. Finishing touches included trim and pediments for windows and doors and a round, coloured-glass window showing the Salvation Army crest. In a dome at the crossing of the transepts and nave hangs a large gasolier from the 1880s. It holds six kerosene lamps, and, while it is not an original fixture, it is typical of those used in the churches of the region at the turn of the century. Its lamps are electric, and reproduction wall brackets positioned along the sidewalls of the nave hold similarly electrified oil lamps. Bulbs recessed in the ceiling provide auxiliary light.

The new basement contains a kitchen, washroom, and meeting hall. It was finished in a modern style, with no attempt to recreate the atmosphere of the period when the original building was constructed.

During the summer of 1976, exterior painting was completed, and the overall impression today at Glen Vowell is one of a building that has aged gracefully and suffered no major changes.

Finished interior at Glen Vowell

Glen Vowell Citadel after restoration

Glossary

APSE. A semicircular or polygonal recess in a church.

BALLOON FRAME. A frame for a wooden building constructed from many regularly spaced small timbers.

BALL-TURNED. Carved in the shape of a ball on a wood-turning lathe.

BALUSTER. A support for a railing.

BALUSTRADE. A railing composed of posts (*balusters*) and a handrail.

BARGEBOARD. A board, usually decorated, fixed to the edge of a *gabled roof*.

BARREL VAULT. A curved ceiling.

BASE BLOCKS. See *blocks*.

BAY. A window or a door, comprising one visual division of a *facade*.

BEADING. Small projecting molding of rounded surface, continuous or broken.

BELFRY. A *cupola* made to contain a bell.

BELLCAST ROOF. A roof that curves outwards towards its lower part, like the flanges of a bell.

BLIND ARCADE. An arcade immediately in front of a wall where the arches are decorative only.

BLOCKS. Rectangular pieces of wood, usually decorated, used as head, corner, or base blocks in constructing window and door frames. See also *quoin*.

BOARD-AND-BATTEN. A wall covering constructed of broad vertical boards whose joints are covered by narrow vertical strips of wood.

BOSS. A projecting ornamental form.

BUILDERS' PAPER. Paper used for insulation in walls, roofs, or between floors.

BULL'S EYE WINDOW. A circular window, usually centred in a *facade*.

BUTT HINGE. A hinge mounted flush into the edge of a door and the face of the casing against which the edge of the door butts when closed.

BUTTRESS. A *pier* applied to the wall of a building. Buttresses may reinforce the walls structurally, or they may be used purely as a decorative element of the *Gothic Revival style*.

CAPITAL. The top portion of a column, usually ornamental.

CHAIR RAIL. A line of *molding* at the top of a *dado*.

CHAMFER. A slanting or bevelled edge, made by cutting off a square edge or corner at an angle.

CHANCEL (sanctuary). The portion of a church containing the altar.

CHROMOLITHOGRAPH. A colour picture or print made from a flat, specially prepared stone or metal plate.

CLAPBOARD. See *siding*.

CLERESTORY. In a church building, a row of windows located near the top of a wall.

CLERGY STALL. A fixed enclosed seat in the choir or *chancel* of a church for the use of the clergy.

COLONNADE. A row of columns.

CORBEL. A kind of wall bracket helping to support a projecting ledge above it.

CORNER BLOCKS. See *blocks*.

CORNICE. An ornamental projecting *molding* along the top of a wall or building.

COVE SIDING. See *siding*.

CRENELLATED PARAPET. A *parapet* with indentations like those in battlements.

CRESTING. Decoration along the ridge of a roof; often a row of *finials*, and often made of *fretwork*.

CROCKET. An ornament, usually made to imitate curved and bent foliage, running up the edge of a *gable*.

CRUCIFORM. In the form of a cross.

CUPOLA. A small, often domed, turret on top of a building.

DADO. The lower part of an inside wall which has been treated decoratively.

DENTIL CORNICE. A *cornice* composed of a *molding* above and a row of tooth-like blocks below.

DORMER. A window projecting from a sloping roof.

DOSSAL. A drapery behind the altar.

DOUBLE-HUNG SASH. A *sash* supported on each side by a counterweighted sash cord or a spring tension device.

DOVETAIL. An interlocking joint formed by corresponding projections and openings, as in the corners of hewn log buildings.

DRUM. The walls of a *spire* or *belfry* which contain the opening for the sound of the bell.

EAVES. The part of a roof between the walls and the roof edge where a roof overhangs the walls of the building.

FACADE. The front part of a building.

FINIAL. An ornament at the top of a roof or decorating the top of any item, such as a tower corner or a pew.

FLUSH-MOUNTING HINGE. A hinge mounted on the broad surface of a door or window, joining it to the adjacent surface of the door or window frame.

FRETWORK. Elaborate wooden decoration cut with a fretsaw or a bandsaw.

FRIEZE. A horizontal decorative band around a room or building.

GABLE. The triangular portion of a wall at the end of a pitched roof.

GABLED ROOF. A roof that slopes on two sides.

GEORGIAN STYLE. An architectural style of the Georgian period (named after the four English King Georges reigning between 1714 and 1830). It was characterized by the forms of ancient Greece and Rome.

GOTHIC REVIVAL STYLE. An architectural style based on the building forms of the Middle Ages, usually used for churches, and characterized by pointed arches and vertical lines.

HAMMERBEAM ROOF. An elaborate system of beams allowing an open ceiling, not frequently used except in large stone buildings.

HEAD BLOCKS. See *blocks*.

HERRINGBONE. Arranged in a zigzag pattern.

KEYSTONE. The middle stone at the top of an arch that holds the other stones or pieces in place. In a wooden building, a block of wood may be used to imitate a keystone.

LATTICE. A structure of crossed wooden or metal strips with open spaces between them.

LECTERN. A reading desk in a church, especially the desk from which the lessons are read at daily prayer.

LOUVRES. Horizontal strips of wood set slanting in an opening, so as to keep the rain out but provide ventilation.

LOZENGE FRIEZE. A *frieze* decorated with diamond shapes, usually at the top of a wall.

LUNETTE. A semicircular or crescent-shaped space or panel, hence a fan-shaped window.

LYCH GATE. A roofed gate to a churchyard.

MILLWORK. Manufactured wooden finishing components used in building.

MOLDING. A shaped strip of wood, often placed around the upper walls of rooms. Usually ornamental, it often conceals joints.

MORTICE-AND-TENON. A joint made by fitting a piece of wood with a projection (tenon) into a slot (mortice) in another piece of wood. Now essentially a cabinetmaker's rather than a carpenter's joint.

MULLION. A bar between the panes of a window, mainly vertical, sometimes curved.

NAVE. The main portion of a church, where the congregation is seated.

NICHE. A recess in a wall for a statue or other object.

NIMBUS. A light disc or halo surrounding a sacred person or thing.

OGEE. A double or s-shaped curve created by joining a concave and a convex curve.

PALLADIAN WINDOW. A window in the form of an arch with two additional, narrow, flat-headed side compartments.

PAPERBOARD. A thick stiff cardboard composed of layers of paper or paper pulp compressed together.

PARAPET. A portion of a wall that projects above a roof.

PARIAN WARE. A hard white porcelain used mainly for making statuettes.

PEDIMENT. The broad triangular end of a *gable* or a triangular element resembling it, on the front of a building.

PIER. A square or rectangular upright post.

PILASTER. A decorative column applied to a wall.

PINNACLE. A slender turret, often only decorative.

PLINTH. The lower square member of the base of a column immediately above ground, or any rectangular base.

POLYCHROME. Decorated with many colours.

POST-AND-BEAM. A building system emphasizing regular use of horizontal and vertical structural members.

QUATREFOIL. An ornamental form composed of four lobes.

QUOIN. A cornerstone or block forming an outside angle at the junction of two walls.

RAFTER. A beam, often slanting, that directly supports the roof of a building.

REEDING. A set of *moldings*, as on a column, resembling small convex fluting.

REREDOS. A decorative wall behind an altar.

ROMANESQUE STYLE. An architectural style characterized by round arches and vaults, based on the heavy masonry building forms prevalent between the ninth and twelfth centuries.

ROOD SCREEN. A screen dividing the *nave* from the *chancel*.

ROSE WINDOW. A circular window, especially one with a pattern radiating from the centre.

SACRISTY (vestry). A room for storing church vestments and altar cloths.

SADDLE NOTCH. A method of joining wall timbers at the corners of simple buildings. Notches on each timber interlock with corresponding notches in the timbers at right angles to it.

SANCTUARY (chancel). The portion of a church containing the altar.

SASH. A fixed or movable framework, as in a window or door, in which panes of glass are set.

SCISSOR TRUSS. A simple but strong crisscross arrangement of *rafters*, making a high, open ceiling possible.

SHED ROOF. A roof that slopes in one direction only.

SHIPLAP. See *siding*.

SIDING. The outer layer applied to a wooden building for weatherproofing and appearance. There are several traditional types, but cove siding is the most common. With this type, horizontal boards overlap each other, and the upper edge of each board has a cove, or concave curve, cut from it. Clapboard is bevelled siding; tongue-and-groove siding consists of boards that fit together by means of corresponding tongues and grooves; shiplap siding is made of boards with notched edges that interlock; board-and-batten siding is constructed of vertical boards whose joints are covered by narrow strips, or battens.

SLAB DOOR (flush door). A door with a flush surface that is not divided into panels and moldings.

SPANDREL. The triangular space between the curve of an arch and the rectangular *molding* or framework that encloses the arch.

SPINDLE. A decorative bar in a railing, usually turned on a lathe.

SPIRE. A steep-sided slender roof coming to a point at the top, often round or polygonal in cross section, usually mounted above a *drum* on a tower.

STATIONS OF THE CROSS. Fourteen scenes from the Passion of Christ, usually painted or sculptured and ranged around the walls of a Roman Catholic church.

STRING COURSE. A projecting horizontal band of decorated *moldings* on the exterior of a building.

STUDS. Slender, upright members of wood forming the frame of a wall or partition to which boards are nailed in making walls.

SUBFLOOR. Boards or sheet material beneath a finished floor.

TABERNACLE. An ornamental receptacle for the safe-keeping of the consecrated elements.

TIE BAR. A horizontal timber, piece of metal, rope, or wire, serving as a tie connecting two structural members to keep them from spreading apart.

TONGUE-AND-GROOVE. A method of joining pieces of wood by means of a strip, or tongue, of wood on one piece that fits into a groove in the other piece. See also *siding*.

TRACERY. Decorative window *mullions*, usually in churches of the Gothic and *Gothic Revival style*.

TRANSEPT. The transverse (shorter) portion of a *cruciform* church.

TRANSOM. A window above a doorway.

TREFOIL. An ornamental form characterized by three lobes.

TURNED WORK. Work carved on a wood-turning lathe, producing cylindrical or molded shapes, often used for handrails and *balusters*.

VERANDA. A large porch along one or more sides of a house.

VESTRY (sacristy). A room for the storage of vestments and altar cloths.

WAINSCOT. A wooden skirting on a wall.

For Further Reading

J. W. ARCTANDER. *The Apostle of Alaska; The Story of William Duncan of Metlakatla.* New York: 1909.
A biased but useful early account of Duncan's work. It is interesting for its expression of the missionary frame of mind.

KENNETH CLARK. *The Gothic Revival.* 1928. Reprint. Harmondsworth: 1962.
A classic in its field, examining the principal ideas and personalities associated with the Gothic Revival in England.

W. H. COLLISON. *In the Wake of the War Canoe.* London: 1915.
Collison's account of Anglican missionary work on the north coast, especially in the Queen Charlotte Islands.

KAY CRONIN. *Cross in the Wilderness.* Vancouver: 1960.
One of the very few recent books on the Oblates of Mary Immaculate in British Columbia. Popular rather than scholarly in its approach.

THOMAS CROSBY. *Up and Down the North Pacific Coast by Canoe and Mission Ship.* Toronto: 1914.
An account of early Methodist missionary work on the north coast.

WILSON DUFF. *The Impact of the White Man. The Indian History of British Columbia.* Vol. 1. Anthropology in British Columbia, Memoir no. 5. Victoria: 1964.
A brief but excellent account of the history of the Indians of British Columbia since the coming of the white man.

ROBIN FISHER. *Contact and Conflict: Indian-European Relations in British Columbia, 1774-1890.* Vancouver: 1977.
Explores the difference between the impact of a fur-trading and a settlement frontier on the Indians. Includes a chapter on the missionaries of the nineteenth century.

GEORG GERMANN. *Gothic Revival: In Europe and Britain: Sources, Influences, and Ideas.* Cambridge, Mass.: 1972.
A useful work, comparing the courses of the Gothic Revival in England, France, and Germany.

SIEGFRIED GIEDION. *Space, Time, and Architecture.* Cambridge, Mass.: 1941.
Particularly valuable for its chapter on the development of American architecture and building technology.

ROBERT F. JORDAN. *Victorian Architecture.* Harmondsworth: 1966.
Considers the architecture of the nineteenth century against the backdrops of romanticism and industrialism. A valuable melding of architectural and social history.

R. G. LARGE. *The Skeena, River of Destiny.* Vancouver: 1957.
A brief history of the north coast with special emphasis on the Skeena Valley.

MARION MacRAE, and ANTHONY ADAMSON. *Hallowed Walls: Church Architecture of Upper Canada.* Toronto: 1975.
An examination of architectural style in the church architecture of early Ontario. Heavily illustrated and competently written.

J. W. W. MOERAN. *McCullagh of Aiyansh.* London: 1923.
An account of the Anglican missionary McCullagh's work among the people of the Nass.

A. G. MORICE. *History of the Catholic Church in Western Canada from Lake Superior to the Pacific (1659-1895).* 2 vols. Toronto: 1910.
While only about a third of the second volume is devoted to British Columbia, the book as a whole provides a useful context for the mission movement in the province.

————. *The History of the Northern Interior of British Columbia.* London: 1906.
Although the period covered (1660-1880) is early in terms of the buildings included in this book, his two chapters on the missionary movement are valuable.

FRANK A. PEAKE. *The Anglican Church in British Columbia.* Vancouver: 1959.
A sympathetic account of the Anglican Church in British Columbia.

JOHN I. REMPEL. *Building with Wood: And Other Aspects of Nineteenth-Century Building in Ontario.* Toronto: 1967.
Well illustrated with both photographs and drawings. Chapters on log construction, frame construction, exterior decoration, and woodworking tools provide a useful background to British Columbian building technology.

JEAN USHER. *William Duncan of Metlakatla: A Victorian Missionary in British Columbia.* National Museum of Man Publications in History, no. 5. Ottawa: 1974.

The best account to date of William Duncan and his work at Metlakatla. Particularly detailed on Duncan's background and the nature of the Metlakatla experiment.

JOHN DE VISSER and HAROLD KALMAN. *Pioneer Churches*. Toronto: 1976.
Well illustrated and written in a popular vein. Considers pioneer church architecture in many parts of Canada and the United States.

H. S. WELLCOME. *The Story of Metlakahtla*. London: 1887.
A completely laudatory and uncritical account of Duncan, written by one who met him.

JAMES F. WHITE. *The Cambridge Movement, The Ecclesiologists and the Gothic Revival*. Cambridge: 1962.
A landmark study, scholarly but readable, and indispensable to an understanding of the Oxford and Cambridge Movements.

List of Churches

DATE DUE
